PRADO MUSEUM
FOREIGN PAINTING

Text: XAVIER COSTA CLAVELL

Photographs, lay-out, reproduction, printing and binding, entirely designed and created by the Technical Department of F.I.S.A.

1st Edition, October 1977

I.S.B.N. 84-378-0021-8

Esp. /Rúst. 84-378-0307-1	Esp. /Lujo 84-378-0311-X
Fran. /Rúst. 84-378-0309-8	Fran. /Lujo 84-378-0313-6
Ing. /Rúst. 84-378-0310-1	Ing. /Lujo 84-378-0314-4
Alem./Rúst. 84-378-0308-X	Alem./Lujo 84-378-0312-8

Dep. Legal B. 30556-XX

editorial escudo de oro, s.a. Palaudarias, 26 - Barcelona, 4 - Spain

Impreso en España - Printed in Spain

PROLOGUE

Works by painters from schools other than the Spanish school are as important a part of the Prado collection as those by our own painters. If it is impossible to become acquainted with Spanish painting and to appreciate the works of El Greco, Velázquez, Ribera and Murillo and especially Goya, without a visit to the Prado, it is equally difficult to get to know or really understand the significance of the art of Hieronymus Bosch, Titian or Rubens, the Flemish painters – from the primitives to Rubens' magnificent contemporaries–, the XVI century Venetians or the painting of Mengs... This is because the nucleus of the Prado collection is made up of paintings from the Spanish Royal House whose monarchs from both the Hapsburg and Borbon dynasties were all fond of the arts, many of them being patrons of the best artists of the time and some, enthusiastic collectors.

The Emperor Charles V's favourite painter was Titian, an eminence in his day; his son Philip II continued to acquire works by Titian and founded a large collection in the Palace of El Escorial and in others of his Palaces. Philip III witnessed the arrival in Spain of Rubens and commissioned paintings by him acquiring whole collections with which to decorate his residences. His son, Philip IV, was one of the most enthusiastic collectors ever to exist and had Velázquez and Rubens, two of the greatest painters of all time, at his service. Monarchs and high dignitaries gave or bequeathed him an infinite number of masterpieces – works by Raphael, Dürer, Titian, Correggio, many more by Rubens, and works by Van Dyck. His son and heir to the throne, the unfortunate Charles II, often rallied his vacilating will power to defend the artistic patrimony he had inherited.

After the introduction of the new Borbon dynasty, high quality French paintings and works of art arrived in vast quantities. The art collections grew and prevailing taste became modified. The king and his wife, queen Isabel Farnese, acquired from Italy and Flanders paintings by contemporary artists and by artists hitherto not represented in the royal collections, and also many French painters worked at Court. Their sons Ferdinand VI and Charles III augmented the collections and summoned many of the greatest artists of the time to Madrid to decorate the New Palace, these were.

Amiconi, Corrado Giaquinto, J.B. Tiepolo among the Italian painters, and the first great neoclassical painter, the German A.R. Mengs. Charles IV whose reign was the epitome of decadence has an important point in his favour in that he was the patron of Goya. An inveterate collector, he gathered together in Rome when he resided there during his old age, a private collection of a thousand paintings. Ferdinand VII acquired some important works for the museum which he had founded with the royal collections, and this unrivalled assembly of paintings was saved by Isabel II who agreed to pay compensation to her sister in order to keep the great inherited collection whole in the Prado Museum. Later, the Museum became nationalized and has continued to acquire more works, its unique nucleus, however, having been provided by the Royal Collection.

It must be added that the present collection is only a part of what the Spanish Royal House acquired and possessed. First of all, fires, among them the terrible one of 1734, which destroyed a third of the collection in the Alcázar, then the Napoleonic invasion with losses due to war and to the greed of the invador that reduced the collection still further.

But what can now be seen in the Prado Museum is an exceptional collection in any sense of the word; it is unique in the beauty of the works exhibited there. The collection has had a long history and is the fruit of the enthusiasm for collecting and the sure and refined taste for pictorical works of art of the Spanish monarchs and their closest advisors during the course of more than four centuries.

This book is a well thought out and simply expressed commentary on the different schools of foreign painting in the Prado Museum along with splendid photographs of its most outstanding and famous works of art.

Xavier de Salas
Director of the Prado Museum

THE ITALIAN SCHOOL

Italian painting is of outstanding importance within the framework of universal art. With the Renaissance, beginning its initial phase in the so called "Quattrocento" (XV century) and reaching the zenith of its splendour in the XVI century, Italy was for some time in the forefront as an exponent of the plastic arts. Coinciding with the spirit of renovation which inspired society at the time, a period of struggle to penetrate the mists of mediaevalism and to reach the bright sunlight of Greco-Latin antiquity was taking place, and in Italy this produced the flowering of Renaissance art. The Italian artist was a person stimulated by a constant creative urge, ever seeking new forms of expression and succeeding in reaching the height of artistic achievement. He was constantly searching, and his discoveries encouraged him to continue his search. On contemplating this enormous artistic movement in retrospect, XX century man cannot help but be impressed. Really one should not speak of an Italian school. Rather should we refer to the Tuscan school — with Masaccio the "Initiator", considered to be the first "cursed artist" —, the Venetian school, with its Byzantine influence, a true apotheosis of colour — the schools of Padua and of Ferrara... In this text we use the expression *Italian school* in its wider sense, without any attempt to dogmatize and being well aware of its ambiguity, to refer collectively to the painters born in Italy whose works hang in the Prado Museum. All of them are of great interest, and some — Mantegna, Botticelli, Raphael, Tintoretto and Titian, are among the most celebrated. If, during the greater part of the *Quattrocento,* the most outstanding painters in the history of art — Botticelli, Bellini, for example, behaved in real life like craftsmen, with an enchanting humility as if anaware of their own value and of the inspiring times they lived in, there were other painters, both in the XV and XVI centuries, who were of a more dominating character with a clearly defined aura of masterful genius — Leonardo da Vinci, Michael Angelo and Raphael for example.

"The golden age of Italian art, the *Cinquecento* (XVI century) said Elie-Charles Flamand, was the natural evolution and complete development of the *Quattrocento.* But the "maniera grande" (grand manner) of the XVI century artists differed markedly from the "rather hard and slightly crude manner" of their predecessors. Less ingenuous and more cultured, the painters of the XVI century were not attracted by anecdotic elements or amusing detail. Anything not purely relevant to the essential theme of the picture was discarded. In future, simplicity and clarity were to be the predominant characteristics of composition, and each element in the picture organized so as to achieve an overall balance and unity. Under the influence of Neo-Platonic spiritualism, the impressions of the senses were subjected to the rule of the spirit.

The study of human anatomy became fundamental and its depiction reached a perfection which will never be equalled. Enlarged to fill the whole canvas, bodies were powerful in movement with decisive attitudes; passions were however depicted with restraint. From that time on there became evident a certain reserve and even solemnity characterizing the "classical seriousness". On the other hand, an open sensuality was introduced to which the Venetian school was to add its exaltation of Nature. From a technical point of view the foreshortening was more daring and aerial perspective reached its uttermost limits. Figures evolved with perfect fluidity in airy spaces in which the painter, by means of a judicious placing of light, shade, and half light, brought objects nearer or made them appear more distant at will".

This "classical seriousness" in XVI century Italian painting — the period to which the majority of the Italian works on show in the Prado Museum belong — was to remain almost unchanged until Goya and finally another Spaniard, Picasso, brought it to an end in the XX century.

Saint Eloy at the workshop of a silversmith, by Tadeo Gaddi.

Fra Angelico's luminous colours show up clearly in
The Annunciation, one of his loveliest paintings
exhibited in the Prado.

FRA ANGELICO

Giovanni da Fiesole, known in the history of painting by the
name of Fra Angelico (and also Fra Beato and Fra Giovanni)
was one of the most typical representatives of the first half
of the XV century. "In the convent of St. Mark in Florence,
under the pure light of this Tuscan sky that looks like the
image of eternity, writes Henri Focillon in his *"Art d'Occident",* it could be said that Fra Angelico, gifted with the
privilege of a perpetual childhood, was not of his time. Nevertheless, he was not unaware of the discoveries of his century and took advantage of them. But his paintings and even
his frescoes could be considered to be the loveliest miniatures of the Mediaeval period, and, in his profound peace-
fulness, rich symbolism, and shining airy quality, he belonged
to a time more ancient than his dates suggest."

Fra Angelico was born in Vicchio (Tuscany) in 1387 and died
in 1455. Apparently his fondness for painting began during
childhood. Giorgio Vasari the XVI century painter and architect who wrote biographies of the most important figures in
Renaissance art, says that Fra Angelico had already given
evidence of his artistic ability before he took Holy Orders at
the age of twenty. Little is known of his early life. One sup-
poses it to be prematurely imbued with subtle extasy and
devoted to religious contemplation if the basic theme of his
work is to be taken into consideration.

It was when he was living in the sheltered atmosphere of the convent that Fra Angelico began to paint his delightful miniatures, apparently under the direction of a Dominican. As a painter, he was always worthy of his artistic pseudonym. His saintly temperament, given to inner contemplation, was constantly projected in his works which appeared impregnated with mysticism and meekness. All his painting was redolent of spiritual peace and the promise of an after-life of blessedness. There is not the slightest shadow of metaphysical uncertainty in any of Fran Angelico's work. Rather, he seems to enjoy here below and in advance, the eternal happiness to which he was destined.

As a young painter, he felt isolated and fearful of the turbulent atmosphere of the times. The struggle between the two Popes, John XXII, who was deposed, and Gregory XII who abdicated, the Venetian war against Turkey, and revolts breaking out in all parts, caused Fra Angelico to flee the world and take refuge in the convent at Fiesole. This occurred around 1418 when he began to paint several frescoes and works in distemper. His technique for the latter was acquired from the study of the works of Giotto, the great XIV century painter who possibly also influenced him in the simplicity and purity of his excellent frescoes. In 1436, Fra Angelico decorated the convent of San Marcos and carried out several commissions for Cosme dei Medici in the church of the Annunziata in Florence. There are many artistic remains in the Tuscan capital of Fra Angelico's stay there.

Called to Rome by the Pope, Fra Angelico decorated the papal chapel in the Palace of St. Peter. These paintings representing the lives of St. Stephen and St. Lawrence are still preserved albeit in a very bad state.

There exists an anecdote which well illustrates the humility

The seraphic dreams of Fra Angelico make an artistic creation with a deliciously ingenuous, typically mediaeval flavour. In these fragments of the engraving alluding to *The Annunciation-Nativity* and *The Betrothal of the Virgin*, the painter has made a valuable contribution to his *Quattrocento* style creations which are some of the most interesting among the Italian primitives on show in the Prado Museum.

5

The Adoration of the Child Jesus, another of Fra
Angelico's paintings on show in the Prado Museum.

of Fra Angelico's character, that took place almost at the end
of his life. Pope Nicholas V, had, in 1447, commissioned him
to decorate the cathedral of Orvieto. The Pope was delight-
ed with his work on the church and, as a token of apprecia-
tion, decided to elevate him to the position of bishop. The
meek and timid Fra Angelico must have had quite a fright
when he learned of the Pontiff's intention. Nothing was more
contrary to his nature than the glitter and vanity so attractive
to the high Italian clergy in those times. Thus, in keeping
with his character, the artist begged Nicholas V to make
any other clergyman a bishop, as he would not have been
able to take on the grave responsabilities of such an office.
Fra Angelico continued to paint the cathedral of Orvieto
whose decoration was later finished off by Signorelli, and
was engaged in decorating the chapel of Eugene IV when
he died in Rome in 1455.
Among his work in the Prado Museum, *The Annunciation* is
outstanding. "The beauty of this work, said Eugenio D'Ors
in his *"Three Hours in the Prado Museum",* has two levels.
At the first level, a sensation of divine simplicity, ingenuous-
ness, limpid delicacy, clarity, sweetness, humble emotion
and purity can be appreciated. At the second, deeper values

are brought into play. Where at one moment we are be-
witched by childhood, at the next, we are dignified by the
supreme lesson of wisdom".
D'Ors, who considered this picture the best of those belonging to the school of Italian primitives in the Prado Museum,
added: "Now we can begin to understand, for example, that
colour in painting may be something very different from
light, and each may possess almost contradictory qualities.
Fra Angelico was not a painter who specialized in colour, he
was not avid for subject matter, he was a luminous painter,
thirsty for the soul. An artist in colour works so as to make
things throb with the exhilaration of the moment; an artist
in light endeavours to depict things in a tranquil state, in
their position in eternity. In the Luxemburg museum in Paris,
the Impressionists belonging to the Caillebote legacy are
becoming blackened and sadly spoilt year by year, by contrast, how constantly fresh and what a golden youthfulness
is to be found in *The Annunciation,* yesterday, today, and
forever!"
What could be refered to as the angelic subject matter in
The Annunciation is captivatingly situated in the world of
Nature with an all pervading magic mysticism.

MANTEGNA

Andrea Mantegna was born in 1431 in Isola di Cartura near Padua, and died in Mantua in 1506. He was only ten years old when he was adopted by maestro Squarcione, in whose studio in Padua Mantegna began his career as an artist. Later his work underwent the influence of Andrea de Castagno, Paolo Uccello, and Donatello.

Mantegna married a daughter of Jacopo Bellini's in Venice when he was twenty three. Well versed in the history of ancient times, he began to paint subjects related to Roman classicism. He developed later and became a brilliant reformer of the Italian painting of his period. Mantegna was the first painter to refuse to paint within the aesthetic norms of the Gothic "devotion" then so popular in northern Italy. His influence on Italian painting was appreciable. Mantegna took part, from 1454 to 1459, in the frescoe decoration of the Ovetari chapel in the Eretimani church, and in 1488 commissioned by Innocent VIII, he decorated the Chapel of the Belvedere in Rome. He was also responsible for the decoration of the Camera degli Sposi in the Old Palace at Mantua and for the frieze named *The Triumph of Julius Caesar,* measuring twenty seven metres which he was commissioned to do for a theatre.

The Death of the Virgin, a painting by Mantegna on show in the Prado, attracts our attention by the strength of its expression and the precisión of its composition.

In *The Death of the Virgin,* Andrea Mantegna reveals the precision characteristic of this typical example of the painting of the *Quattrocentro.*

The Virgin between two Saints, the work of Giovanni Bellini (1436-1516), a painter of the Venetian School who specialized in religious subjects.

7

BOTTICELLI

Alessandro di Mariano Filippepi, which was Botticelli's real name, was, without any doubt, one of the Italian Renaissance painters whose popularity has been paramount and continues to be so at the present time. Botticelli was born in Florence in 1444 and died there in 1510. He was the pupil of a goldsmith, and began his education as an artist in the studio of Fra Filippo Lippi, where he started work at the age of fifteen. Later he had lessons form Antonio Pollaiuolo who familiarized him with the new pictorial tendencies in Italy at the time.

In 1470 he painted, in the Palace della Mercantazia in his native city, a panel called *Fortezza,* and his name began to appear form 1472 beside those of the great masters of the Florentine school. In 1480, Botticelli was commissioned by Lorenzo the Magnificent to paint the work entitled *Pallas taming the Centaur,* an allegory of the diplomatic victory gained by the Medici over Naples. He also painted three motifs for the decoration of the Sixtine Chapel in Rome. He illustrated Dante's *Divine Comedy* and, under the influence of the empassioned speech of the visionary Savonarola, he abandoned painting and took his own pictures to be burned in the bonfire of vanities at the Carnival of 1497. He carried on painting after Savonarola's death, but his work was of an appreciably lesser quality. His name remained in eclipse for several centuries, but in mid XIX century, thanks to the enthusiasm with which Ruskin praised his work, the name of Botticelli began to recoup its lost popularity.

Perhaps his most famous paintings are *The Birth of Venus,* and *Spring,* both of which are kept in the Ufizzi gallery in Florence. The winged beauty of these paintings seems to re-live convicingly in these verses dedicated to Botticelli by Rafael Alberti:

> La Gracia que se vuela,
> que se escapa en sonrisa,
> pincelada a la vela,
> brisa en curva deprisa,
> aire claro de tela
> alisada,
> concisa,
> céfiros blandos en camisa,
> por el mar, sobre el mar,
> todo rizo huidizo,
> torneado ondear,
> rizado hechizo...

In *The Story of Nastasio degli Honesti,* a painting now in the Prado, Botticelli paints with an overflowing lyricism and gives a magnificent example of his refined artistic sensibility.

This is the first of the paintings by Sandro Botticelli describing *The History of Nastasio degli Honesti.*

In these two works the artist continues and finishes *The History of Nastasio degli Honesti,* these paintings combine a freshness of colour with an intense lyricism characteristic of the best of Botticelli's works.

TITIAN

Even now it has been impossible to establish the date of Vecellio Tiziano's birth. The date generally accepted nowadays is between 1488 and 1490. There is, however, no doubt about where he was born—in Piave di Cadore—, a town where several generations of his ancestors had lived and where Titian's father was a magistrate. Titian's family were of aristocratic descent. One of his grandfathers bore the title of count and was a notary public and advocate. He had six children and among his grandchildren were two painters, Titian and Marco Vecellio, who were cousins.

Marcel Brion wrote the following lines about Titian's first steps in his artistic career: "There is little to say of his first apprenticeship in the studio of a more or less obscure master, Sebastiano Zuccato. However, he learned a great deal from the teacher who received him on leaving Zuccato, for Giovanni Bellini, as Dürer said admiringly, "was still the greatest painter in Venice"; in Bellini's studio the young apprentice met Giorgione, who possessed all the necessary qualities to fascinate an adolescent with the promise of future genius, and also that inimitable something only he had and which no one dared to copy".

In 1508, Titian, in collaboration with Giorgione painted the fresco on the German Commercial Exchange (Fondaco dei Tedeschi) on the Rialto bridge. In their early works, both were profoundly influenced by Bellini and their style was very similar, although Giorgione and Titian were very different in personality and sensibility.

Giorgione was older than Titian and quite naturally felt himself to be the master, considering the younger man a gifted pupil. Nevertheless, people had it that Giorgione soon became jealous of Titian. Vasari states that the latter showed off one of his frescoes and the praise he received annoyed Giorgione so much that he decided to stop working with him.

In 1513, Cardinal Pietro Bembio invited Titian to accept the post of painter to the pontifical court in Rome, but he refused. 1516 was an important year in Titian's life as it was the time when he came into contact with the duke of Ferrara, Alfonso I d'Este, the Renaissance prince enamoured of the arts who felt it his duty to act as a patron. During this period, Titian painted the portrait of Ludovico Ariosto and *The Bacchanal* which hangs in the Prado. In 1523, Titian met the marquis of Mantua, Federico Gonzaga, and from then of there began a brilliant period in Titian's art. Among the pictures he painted for Gonzaga is the one entitled *Young Woman combing her Hair,* which is now in the Louvre.

The painter's youth was characterized by a complete freedom in his amorous persuits. He had more than one mistress and

A magnificent *Self-Portrait,* possibly the last to be painted by Titian.

his wife Cecilia whom he married in 1525 had lived with him previously, bearing him two sons Pomponio and Orazio. Titian was a great friend of the daring, intelligent Aretino, and it is quite possible that the latter influenced in certain characteristics of Titian's painting, especially the subject matter. It must be noted that Titian was one of the painters most fond of the female nude, although in the bodies and the poses depicted on his canvases there is not the same amorous ardour as that expressed in the writings of the author of the *Ragionamenti.*

Philip II, Federico Gonzalo I Duke of Mantua, The Empress Isabel of Portugal and *The Emperor Charles V on horseback,* these are four examples of Titian's exceptional gifts as a portrait painter.

Two magnificent Virgins ("La Dolorosa"), showing
Titian's mastery of the art of painting.

In 1530, Titian began to be connected with the Spanish court,
painting his first portrait of Charles V. Made a Count Pala-
tine by him in 1533, he became the Emperor's official painter.
Titian's work, one of the most outstanding in the Renaissance
period, is well represented in the Prado Museum. There are
thirty six paintings by the great Italian master, among them
perhaps the most worthy of mention being the following:
Charles V at the Battle of Mühlberg, a vast canvas (332 ×
279), which took the artist half a year to paint (1548), and
which without any doubt is one of Titian's best works, *Danae
receiving the Golden Rain,* a work belonging to the collec-

Saint Marguerite, one of the many paintings by Titian
in the Prado Museum.

The Adoration of the Kings, and The Burial of Christ —two paintings which although depicting a much treated subject, show Titian's praiseworthy vigour of artistic expression. They evidence an intelligent, functional use of colour and a masterly architectural orderliness in composition which are two of his salient characteristics.

tion Of so-called "poems" that Titian painted for Philip II before he acceded to the throne of Spain; *Venus enjoying Music,* a work of great beauty throbbing with the atmosphere of Venice, even in the pearly feminime flesh whose curves exude a delicate erotism very typical of the Renaissance, *Self-Portrait,* possibly Titian's last picture, painted around 1567, in this the painter wears a grave expression as though he were aware that his end was near, an irrepressible melancholy pervades his image, accentuated pictorically by what looks like a halo round the artist's head composed of light and shade, reminiscent of the subtle use of colour in the best of Rembrandt's work, *Portrait of Philip II,* a flat-tering study of the Prince which, although splendidly executed and in magnificent colour, is somewhat artificial in its composition, *Portrait of the Empress Doña Isabel of Portugal, St. Marguerite, the Adoration of the Kings, The Mater Dolorosa, The burial of Christ,* and *Bacchanal.*

Danae, one of Titian's most interesting works on mythological subjects. This painting belongs to the collection of so-called "poems" painted for Philip II before his accession to the throne of Spain.

This lovely nude - *Venus enjoying Music*, with its slightly artificial composition, is less sensual than others of Titian's nudes such as *Danae*, *The Urbino Venus*, or *Venus* which are also in the Prado Museum.

In this work, *The Bacchanal*, Titian shows a dramatic intensity which contrasts with the classic serenity of his earlier paintings.

In his magnificent picture *The Virgin with The Child in arms between St. Anthony of Padua and St. Roque*, Giorgione gives an example of his desire for artistic perfection. There is an admirable balance between the exactitude of the colours and the predominating shadows, and a smooth elegance in the outline of the figures which are beautifully executed.

In The Adoration of the Shepherds by Palma the Elder, "a painting so dark and so clear at the same time", there appears that "subterranean gold", that lighted lamp spoken of by Eugenio D'Ors in his book *Three hours in the Prado Museum*.

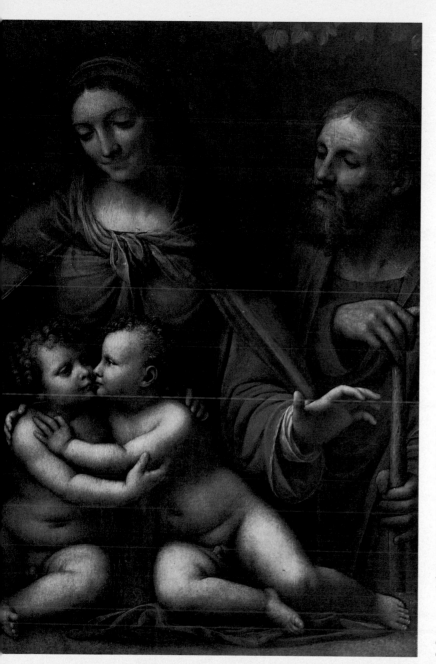

Bernardino Luini, a painter born in Luino on the shores of Lake Maggiore circa 1480, and who probably died in Milan in 1532, produced paintings which were clearly influenced by the style of Leonardo da Vinci. Even his subjects were of the type characteristic of Leonardo's aesthetic and he also used the sfumato technique. But the faces drawn by Luini although possessing some of the delicate elegance of Leonardo's, have none of that mysterious ambiguity found in the *Mona Lisa* which epitomizes Leonardo's poetic approach. *The Holy Family* by Bernardino Luini, now in the Prado, reveals the artistic qualities of its author it that it is a balanced work as regards composition, with the head of the Virgin surrounded by an evocatively poetic halo.

The Continence of Scipio by Peruzzi is perfect in its execution and at first sight vaguely recalls the genial compositions of Hieronymus Bosch.

RAPHAEL

Raphael "the divine", was born and died on Good Friday. His life cycle took place between two important dates in the religious calender. All his work is likewise imbued with religious motives, with his Virgins, Saints, and Holy Families... Raphael as a painter was a saintly interpreter of divinely inspired conventional beauty. When he died, he was working on a picture of the *Transfiguration* which remained unfinished. Vasari, that incomparable chronicler of Renaissance art and biographer of the great painters who were his contemporaries, said of the author of *The Virgin with the Fish:* "seeing the body dead and the painting alive tears the soul apart with grief".

Raphael is perhaps the most directly responsible for the overflowing of affection represented by manierism. His work was sweetly beautiful and closer to the chromolithographs inspired by the narrow, less distinguished heirs of Renaissance art than to the vigorous creative strength of a Michael Angelo, for example, or the ambiguous poetry of a Leonardo. The work of Raphael is not difficult to assimilate. If trained and able, any mediocre painter could reflect and produce a similar work. But in the copy or the imitation there would certainly be lacking that subtle grace which was the soul of Raphael's work. But his artistic creation will remain. This is what happened to Raphael more than to any other of the great Renaissance artists, with the manierists. Rafael Alberti saw this danger surrounding the type of beauty Raphael created very clearly, as these verses show:

> *De rumor de Amorcillos,*
> *sus plumas enlazadas*
> *a las de las palomas en grecas de frutales,*
> *se ladean los arbolillos,*
> *las cabelleras encintadas*
> *y el aliento de los cendales.*
> *Gracioso manadero*
> *tranquilo, de dulzura,*
> *masculina inocencia femenina.*
> *El aire es venero*
> *de fina arquitectura*
> *y áurea sección divina.*
> *Ungido, preferido*
> *de la delicadeza.*
> *Muda muchacha, la belleza*
> *te da su único vestido.*
> *De rodillas las Gracias te llevan, te llevaron.*
> *Tu alma no yace. Ondea*
> *serenamente y pura*
> *en la sonrisa que dejaron*
> *Venus, Apolo y Galatea*
> *por el cielo de tu pintura.*

His delicate "Heaven of painting", was what dazzled Raphael's imitators who were incapable of penetrating through the formal beauty into the spring of poetry existing in his outstanding creations.

Portrait of a Cardinal is one of Raphael's masterpieces. The composition is a prodigy of harmony and the use of colour perfectly adapted to the psychology reflected in the face of the ecclesiastic.
Everything in this painting has a touch of reality; there are no strident tones nor is there that facility of expression so typical of Raphael. The colour is sober and efficiently expressive, in harmony with the elegant classicism of the composition.

The Virgin with the Rose, a painting by Raphael now in the Prado along with *The Virgin with the Fish* makes up part of the series of Raphael's Madonnas.

Raphael was born in Urbino on April 6th 1483 and died in Rome at the early age of thirty seven. His career in painting began very early. As a young boy he left Urbino, went first to Perusa and Florence and then to Rome in 1509 where he immedietely became the rival of Michael Angelo who, at that time was painting the famous frescoes on the ceiling of the Sixtine Chapel. In 1514, Raphael substituted Bramante as the architect of the Basilica of St. Peter. The artist devoted himself completely to his creative task. During this period of his life, apart from his pictorial work, he also devoted himself to the reconstruction of the Branconio del'Aquila palace and the palace of Caffarelli Vidoni. In 1515 Raphael was commissioned to paint the cartoons for the tapestries in the Sixtine Chapel and was appointed curator of Roman antiquities by the Pope.

The most outstanding work by Raphael in the Prado Museum is the *Portrait of a Cardinal,* a normal sized painting (79 × 62) probably executed between 1510 and 1511. This is certainly one of Raphael's masterpieces. The composition is a prodigy of harmony and the colour perfectly adapted to the psychology reflected by the visage of the cardinal. Everything strikes a note of reality in this picture. There is nothing out of place,

The Holy Family, called *"The Pearl",* and *The Holy Family with the Lamb,* are two works by Raphael in which his inimitable talent for paintings of a religious nature is shown off to perfection.

nor even the usual fluency typical of Raphael in the drawing nor in the colouring which is sober and expressive making an elegantly classical composition. This painting, and the *Portrait of Castiglione* and the *Portrait of Leon X* and other works of the same type with their perfect plasticity and acute psychological penetration represent the greatness of Raphael still capable of resisting the most severe critical analysis. Other works by the same artist in the Prado gallery are: *The Virgin of the Rose, The Virgin with the Fish, The Holy Family with the Lamb,* and several other paintings on this religious theme.

The Holy Family and the Oak Tree - one of Raphael's religious paintings on show in the Prado.

In his painting *Micer Marsilio and his Wife*, Lorenzo Lotto succeeds in subtly and convincingly reflecting the atmosphere of the so-called "drawing-room paintings" which were to enjoy so much standing later.

Christ carrying the Cross by Sebastiano del Piombo (1485-1547), a painter who was born in Venice and who died in Rome where he was appointed Keeper of the Seals by the Pope. He was a friend of Raphael, Michael Angelo and Cellini.

LORENZO LOTTO

Born in Venice in 1480, Lorenzo Lotto died in 1556 in Loreto. This artist, along with Palma the Elder and Paris Bordone, was one of the Renaissance painters whose work most reflected the influence of Titian. Lotto began his career as an artist under the direction of the painter from Murano, Alvise Vivarini. He was summoned to Rome in 1509 by Julius II and lived there until 1512, taking part in the decoration of the Vatican. But his paintings, and also frescoes of other famous artists, were later removed so that Raphael could have room for his works.

Lotto went to Bergamo in 1518 and in that city, where he remained until 1528, ha painted the excellent altar pieces of San Bartolomé, San Bernardino and San Espirito, works which according to Elie-Charles Flamand "had in common a sort of jubilance, an intense liberty of movement and fullness of form manifested in the expressions on the faces which were mystic and voluptuous at the same time".

In 1529 Lorenzo Lotto returned to Venice and had the opportunity of making friends with Titian who was at that time, the most important figure in Venetian painting. Towards the end of his life, he retired to a monastery in Loreto. Among Lotto's best works, those most worthy of mention are — *The Betrothal of St. Catherine, The Triumph of Chastity, St. Nicholas in Heaven* and *St. Jerome in the Desert. Micer Marsilio and his Wife*, on show in the Prado Museum is a good example of the artistic qualities of this painter.

Andrea del Sarto's impeccable mastery of drawing is reflected in this magnificent portrait of *Lucrecia di Baccio del Fede* the balance of the shapes is in harmony with the muted tones of the colouring. "It was for this reason, as Eugenio D'Ors points out, that del Sarto was known in legend as *Andrea senza errori* "(Andrea without mistakes)".

ANDREA DEL SARTO

Born in Florence in 1486, Andrea d'Agnolo was the son of a tailor, which is why the painter had himself called "del Sarto", the name under which he went down in the history of painting. He learnt to draw in the workshop of a goldsmith and afterwards stayed three years with the painter and sculptor Gio Barile. Later on he entered the studio of Piero di Cosimo although his real master was Leonardo da Vinci. Andrea del Sarto was immediately attracted by the *sfumato* technique used by Leonardo, a technique which allowed the painter of *Mona Lisa* to substitute, in the words of Flamand, "the tense drawing of the XV century artists with their hard shapes, arranged in the clear universe of vertical light, by a vaporous model in whom everything melts and becomes diffused, surrounded by an imprecise clarity giving the figures a secret life, which is almost disturbing, filling them with mystery and unattainable poetry".

Andrea del Sarto began to decorate the cloister of the Annunziata in the convent of the servants in 1509. It consisted of a group of frescoes representing five stages in the *Life of St. Philip Benicio,* a curious mediaeval personage, a worker of miracles born in Florence in the XIII century, founder of the Servants of Mary. Del Sarto afterwards painted for the same church another two frescoes entitled *The Journey of the Magi* and *The Birth of the Virgin.* Both these works consolidate the artistic prestige of Andrea d'Agnolo.

In 1514, commissioned by the brotherhood of the "scalzo" he painted a *Life of St. John the Baptist* and the allegorical figures of *Faith, Hope, Charity* and *Justice* to decorate the cloister walls. These works occupied the artist for some 15 years, although it must be said that during that time he painted many other pictures. The aforementioned paintings were done in grisaille and as a whole make up one of the artist's most important creations. "They do not lack variety, comments Flamand, or strength, with their smoke

The Holy Family by Andrea del Sarto on show in the Prado Museum.

The Virgin, the Child, a Saint and an Angel, a painting by Andrea del Sarto also on show in the Prado Museum.

coloured shadows, their slightly reddish blacks, and their white, toned in with yellow, the whole work is in temperate warm harmony. Among the most outstanding are indubitably *The Preaching of St. John,* and *the Baptism of Christ.*

Other interesting frescoes by Del Sarto are those he painted in the Medici villa in 1521, and in the convent of San Solvi in 1526. The first is entitled, *Caesar receiving tribute of animals from Egypt,* a work of great inspiration and with a harmonious architectural perspective, the second is *The Supper,* a work clearly inspired by Leonardo and impregnated with subtle poetry and a vigorous sense of colour.

Although he really belonged to the Florentine school, Venetian infuences are to be observed in Andrea del Sarto in the brightness of his colours. There are also influences of Correggio in his fine, exquisite sensitivity. "The smoothness of his brush-strokes", states Buschel, "is extraordinary. He was the only Florentine who applied paint as they did in Venice; but his colours did not always melt into a homogeneous accord as in the Venetian mode, for often they were juxtaposed". Del Sarto died in Florence in 1530, in despair, it seems, after having been abandoned by Lucrezia del Fede, his wife, a woman of extraordinay beauty and no less frivolity. The painter too was considered by his contemporaries as a rather frivolous and superficial person. Nevertheless, he was sincerely appreciated as an artist.

Among Andrea del Sarto's best work are the following: *The Annunciation, The Betrothal of St. Catherine, Madonna of the Harpies, The Laying in the Tomb, The Legend of Joseph, The Quarrel, Portrait of a Sculptor,* and *Charity.* This last picture was painted by del Sarto during his stay in Fontaine-bleau where he was summoned by Francis I. In the Prado is the lovely portrait of the painter's wife, *The Holy Family* and *The Virgin, a Child, a Saint, and an Angel,* all of which show the undoubted ability of Andrea del Sarto as an artist.

The Adoration of the Shepherds, by Giulio Romano (1499-1546) a painter born in Rome who died in Mantua; he illustrated the famous erotic sonnets of Aretino.

Correggio is represented in the Prado by two paintings, *The Virgin, the Child and St. John* and *Noli me tangere.*

CORREGGIO

Antonio Allegri bore the name of the town, Correggio, in which he was born (1489) and died (1534). The son of a prosperous merchant, Correggio received an appropriate education. He was an apprentice in several studios and in Modena he became the pupil of Bianchi Ferrari.

Correggio painted his first frescoe entitled *The Hunt of Diana,* for the convent of Saint Paul at Parma, where the Abbess carried on a life style which was far from being religious. He afterwars decorated the dome of the church of the fathers of Montecasino at Parma. *The Mystic Marriage of St. Catherine* is Correggio's most famous painting. His work is characterized by its sweetness, poetic charm and a very personalized sensual quality. In the works by Correggio in the Prado Museum—*The Virgin, The Child Jesus and St. John,* we have an excellent example of his delicate artistic sensitivity.

25

Don García de Medici, one of the best portraits painted by Bronzino, the pseudonym used by Agnolo di Cosimo di Mariano, (1503-1572); *Lady with three Children,* a work by Francesco Mazzola (1503-1540) better known by his nickname Parmigianino, alluding to the city of Parma where he was born; *Allegory of the birth of the Infante Don Fernando, son of Philip II* by Parrasio. These three painting are all to be found in the Prado Museum.

JACOPO BASSANO

The Bassanos made up a large family of painters composed of Jacopo, Francesco, Giambattista, Girolamo and Leandro. Jacopo Bassano was the son of Francesco da Ponte the Elder who was his first teacher. He was born in 1510 in the town of Bassano situated on the slopes of the Alps from which he acquired his artistic pseudonym, and died in 1592. Jacopo was for some time at Bonifazio de Pitati's studio in Venice where he got to know Veronese and Tintoretto. Later he returned to Bassano where he spent the rest of his long life. Jacopo Bassano became a specialist in works of a religious nature. He also painted pictures of bucolic and peasant scenes in which he liked to put animals and shepherds in the foreground and fill the background with divine figures as decorative elements.

He was appointed Councellor and Consul of his native town and belonged to the Brotherhood of San Giuseppe, la Scuola del Sacramento and i Battuti. In 1534, he painted *Flight from Egypt* for the church of San Girolamo, decorated a room in the Praetorian Palace between 1535 and 1536, painted the frescoes in the cathedral at Bassano in 1538, a reading room in the Praetorian Palace and several works for the cathedral at Belluno, for churches in Venice and Padua and also for the Ducal Palace. Among his best known painings are those entitled *The Angels' Anunciation to the Shepherds,* and *Departure for Canaan.* In the Prado there is a *Self-Portrait of Jacopo Bassano* and *The Expulsion of the Merchants from the Temple.*

An excellent *Self-Portrait* and *The expulsion of the Merchants from the Temple*, both works by Jacopo Bassano in the Prado. In these paintings it can be easily appreciated that the artist has followed the aesthetic norms of the Venetian school.

In his painting *Judith and Holofernes*, Tintoretto reflects an atmosphere in which the horror of the story appears to be extenuated by the poetic depiction of the night, bathed in a blue light.

TINTORETTO

Born in Venice in 1518, Jacopo Robusti died in the same city in 1594. The son of a dyer which gave the nickname by which he is known in the history of art, he became a pupil of Titian but stayed with him for only a short time. It was said that Titian felt jealous of his young pupil and dismissed him from his studio. Tintoretto's first most important works were, *Adam and Eve* and *The Murder of Abel,* for which he was commissioned by the church of the Holy Trinity. In 1546 he decorated the church of Santa Maria dell'Orto with frescoes and in 1548 the Brotherhood of San Marcos commissioned several paintings on subjects related to their patron saint. Competing with Veronese and other painters, Tintoretto won a competition for the decoration of the new building constructed by the opulent Brotherhood of San Roque. He worked for 23 years on this task, painting sixty two pictures, among them those entitled *Original Sin, Picking up the Manna, The Baptism of Christ, Temptation in the Desert, The Miracle of the Loaves, Prayer in the Orchard,* and *Resurrection.* In 1572 he painted a picture on the *Victory of Lepanto,* oficially commissioned by the Senate of the Venetian Republic.

In the work of Tintoretto, his facet as a splendid portrait painter is also to be emphasized. True masterpieces of this branch of art are his portraits of Henry III, Carlo Morosini, Aloise Mocenigo, Andrea Dandolo and Jacopo Soranzo. His famous *Self Portrait* is also of exceptional value. Towards the end of his life, Tintoretto was commissioned to decorate the great Council Chamber in the Doge's Palace. This was a grandiose work known by the name of *The Glory of Paradise,* an astonishing gallery in which some five hundred people were portrayed.

Tintoretto was an inexaustable worker living exclusively for and by his work. "All we know about him", wrote Adrien Mithouard in 1910 in *Les Marches de l'Occident,* "shows he had an antisocial character. He was eccentric. Never laughed. His replies inhibited any conversation. When the Senators, seeinh him paint some parts of the *Paradise* with great brush strokes, asked him why Giovanni Bellini, by contrast, worked with such care, he replied that it was because he didn't have people around him who irritated him. An important man asked him to decorate his country house; Tintoretto stretched out his arms and placed them against the wall: "How big is it?" — "Three Tintorettos", replied the gentleman. And to Aretino, who always annoyed him whenever he could, on meeting him one day, suggested painting his portrait and took him to his house; once there, Tintoretto took out his pocket pistol. "Don't worry", he said, "it was only to take your measurments: you measure two pistols and a half." Besides being mysterious he was also a joker as can be seen in what happened at San Rocco when, having been asked to submit a sketch for the ceiling of the Sala del'Albergo, he dashed off the finished painting, had it secretly placed on the ceiling and claimed, much to the anger of those present, that he knew of no other way of doing it. Brusqueness and an irritating haughtiness were characteristic of this great man who kept all his strength for the struggle with his art. In his silent anger he is rather similar to Michael Angelo and Beethoven. The distance he always kept between others and himself was what his genius needed in order to excel".

This description of Tintoretto by Mithouard helps us to understand the vigorous work of the cantankerous Venetian painter. Tintoretto needed vast space to paint as he wished. He was attracted by grandiose themes and his torrential inspiration could only express itself freely by painting large canvases. Rafael Alberti aptly defined Tintoretto's creative capacity in these verses.

The Lady baring her breast is a fine portrait of a young Venetian woman in which Tintoretto achieves an elegant, sober and difficult effect with greens and greys.

The Gentleman with the Golden Chain, another of the magnificent portraits by Tintoretto exhibited in the Prado.

Rotos los cielos, rotos.
Sombras despedazadas,
acechadoras luces,
desgarradas.

En la noche, estampidos
solemnes, redoblados,
de los aparecidos
fatigados.

Todo se cae, rueda.
Todo se precipita,
se violenta, se excita.
Y todo queda.

In his painting, *The Lavation,* Tintoretto reveals his absolute mastery of perspective.

The Birth of Christ, by Federico Baroccio (1526-1612), a manierist painter of the schools of Tuscany and Rome in whose work the influence of Corregio and Guido Reni can be observed.

Batalla que reaviva,
reinventa el movimiento
allá en la turbulenta,
turbada, trastornada,
perspectiva del viento.

Apart from the works mentioned previously, a passing reference should be made to his four masterpieces on mythological themes: *Venus joining Bacchus and Ariadne, The Three graces, Pallas rejecting Mars* and *Vulcan's Forge.* Tintoretto reveals his great mastery of the painting of the nude in all these works. "Here, said Flamand, throbbing flesh that seems to absorb light and itself become luminous is enhanced in all its qualities by the intelligent contrast with rich materials or the shine of armour".

Other important works by Tintoretto are those entitled. *St. George fighting the Dragon, The Origin of the Milky Way* and *Susanna in her Bath.*

The following works by Tintoretto are in the Prado Museum: *The Death of Holofernes,* or *Judith and Holofernes,* a particularly fine work; *A Young Venetian Girl,* or *Woman bearing her breast,* with its charmingly sober elegance of expression, a virtuoso piece of colour painting; *The Gentleman with the Golden Chain,* a fine portrait, and *The Lavation* in which the artist shows the complete mastery of perspective characteristic of his painting.

Christ on the Cross, another painting by Baroccio, who was also known as Barocci and Fiori da Urbino, on show in the Prado.

In his painting of *The Holy Family*, Cangiaso Lucca, "Luqueto", achieves a delicately muted atmosphere, and with the subtle expression of the Virgin and the innocent grace of the children, he infuses a certain aura of poetry into the painting.

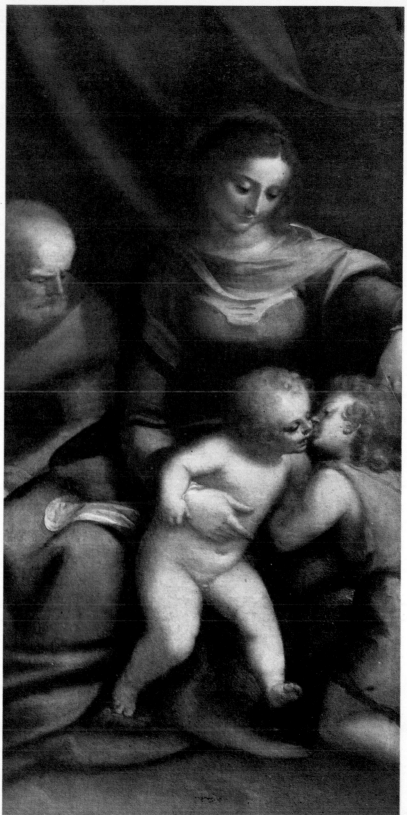

Il Veronese achieves, in his painting *Jesus and the Centurion*, an excellent balance in his use of colour and composition creating a scene of dynamic realism.

VERONESE

Born in Verona in 1528, Paolo Caliari died in Venice in 1588 having become famous under the name alluding to his native town. Veronese is by definition the painter of the Serene Republic of Venice. His work in a way represents a precious example of the fabulous riches of all kinds from both East and West accumulated by Venice throughout the brilliant course of her histoty. Veronese belonged to a family of artists. His father was a sculptor and an uncle of his, Antonio Badile, a painter. It was Veronese's father who initiated him in his chosen profession. Later his uncle orientated his work and afterwards Giovanni Carotto became his master. In association with another young painter, Zelotti, he decorated many palaces and villas. In 1555, Veronese went to Venice and carried out several works commissioned by the prior of the convent of St. Sebastian who also made him undertake the decoration of the church ceiling with the story of Esther. For this same church he also painted the following: *The Annunciation, Prophets, Sibyls, The Martyrdom of St. Sebastian, The Purification of the Virgin, The Sacrificial Bath, The Appearance of the Saint before Diocletian, The Appearance of the Virgin to St. Sebastian, The Martyrdom of St. Sebastian,* and *St. Sebastian exhorting Sts. Marcelo and Marcelino to martyrdom.* In 1562, he painted the famous canvas entitled *The Wedding at Cana* for the convent of St. George The Great. Other famous works by Veronese are,

The Martyrdom of St. Justine for the church in Padua of the same name, *The Rape of Europa, The Triumph of Venice, Military Expeditions by Mocenigo and the Doge Loredano, The Family of Darius at the feet of Alexander after the Battle of Isos* and *The Disciples of Emaus.*

A painter belonging to the Venetian school, Veronese evidenced in his work a strong artistic sensibility with a striking use of colour in which orange and gold tones, bright red and sky blue are particularly outstanding. He is a typical Renaissance artist in subject matter and in style. Alberti has captured with precision Veronese's markedly creative source of inspiration.

> *...Los aires y las flores, como Amores desnudos,*
> *encendidos, veloces por la orilla;*
> *los ropajes, rizados, temblorosos,*
> *colgados de las ramas,*
> *y las sobredoradas palomas de los arcos,*
> *vuelca palmas de luz entre murmullos*
> *de angeles anidados en las nubes.*
> *¡Ven tú, Amor, ancho Amor, ansioso río!*

There are several pictures by Veronese in the Prado: *Vice and Virtue, Cain wandering in the Wilderness, Jesus debating with the doctors, Portrait of Livia Colonna, Portrait of Lavinia Vecellio, Susanna and the Judges, Moses, Jesus at the Wedding at Cana,* and *Jesus and the Centurion.* The latter work shows the artist's mastery of the difficulties of perspective and a balanced use of colour.

In *Moses saved from the waters of the Nile,* Il Veronese reveals the perfection of style characteristic of his art.

Venus and Adonis, by Il Veronese.

The perfect composition and balance of tone in this painting by Il Veronese, *Jesus debating with the Doctors in the Temple,* reveal it as a model of artistic harmony.

The mythological theme of *Venus and Adonis* is ably depicted by Hannibal Carracci (1557-1602) in this painting housed in the Prado Museum.

An atmosphere of impressive realism is created by Caravaggio in his painting *David conquering Goliath.*

CARAVAGGIO

The son of an architect born around 1560 in a village in Lombardy near to Bergamo, called Caravaggio; the painter adopted this as his own name, his real one being Michaelangelo Merisi. Little is known of his youth, but it appears he had an exciting life. He had a turbulent nature and all his life was plagued with adventures, fights, chases and escapes. He began his apprenticeship in Milan and went often to Venice and other cities in Lombardy. He went to Rome in 1590. Up to that time he had lived through all types of difficulties, but he obtained the protection of cardinal Francesco del Monte and painted several pictures for his palace in Rome.

As a consequence of a duel he had to flee to Genoa, and on his return to Rome he killed a man in a brawl and once again had to take to his heels, going into hiding in a small Neapolitan village, Pogliano, where he painted several pictures. Then he went of Malta where the Grand Master of the Order of St. John offered him his protection. Imprisoned after beating up one of the Knights, he was able to escape and take refuge in Sicily. Carrying on painting from church to church between fights, he finally died when he had decided to return to Rome.

Caravaggio was undoubtedly a painter of originality and interest especially when his work is compared to that of the manierists who were his contemporaries. He wanted to be a popular painter and tried to reflect the dynamic reality of life in his works. Even in his paintings of a mythological

Hypomenes and Atalanta, by Guido Reni, an artist who was born in Calvenzano (Bérgamo) in 1575 and who died in 1642 in Bologna. His work was influenced by Caravaggio and Ribera.

In his painting entitled *Victory at Fleurus* in the Prado Museum, Carducho evidenced originality in composition and a meticulous attention to form and use of colour.

nature, such as *David defeating Goliath,* in the Prado, there is an atmosphere of startling realism. Other important works of his are: *Rest during the Flight into Egypt, Bacchus, Basket of Fruit, The Crucifixion of St. Peter, The Holy Burial,* etc.

GUERCINO, GENTILESCHI, FURINI, SACCHI, ROSA...

There are several Italian painters with works in the Prado Museum who, although not very famous, are of undoubted quality. Among these, mention should be made of Giovanni Barbieri, better known as an artist by his pseudonym *il Guernico de Cento (the squint-eyed one from Cento),* a city near Ferrara where he was born in 1591. His painting was evidently influenced by Caravaggio. His frescoes are the most valuable part of his work, among them those decorating the Villa Ludovisi are the most outstanding, especially those entitled *Aurora,* and *Night.* His oil painting is more superficial. A painting of his in the Prado, *Susanna and the Old Men,* shows great artistic vigour. Guercino died in Bologna in 1666.

Another painter of interest is Orazio Gentileschi who was born in Pisa in 1562 and died in London in 1657. Gentileschi went to Rome at a very early age and painted several frescoes there. Those that remain are in a bad state of preservation, but show that Orazio Gentileschi was also influenced by Caravaggio and that he had abandoned the manierist mode at an early stage. In 1626 he went to London at the invitation of Charles I who granted him an income of 500 pounds a year. The pictures he painted in England brought him some fame in Spain, and Philip IV commissioned him to paint *Moses being rescued from the Waters,* now in the Prado. Among his best known works are: *Rest during the Flight into Egypt,* in the Louvre, and *Annunciation,* now in Turin. "Although his naturalism would have been inconceivable had not Caravaggio existed, said Hermann Voss, "the emotional element in Gentileschi is completely different, sweeter, more elegant and lyrical, at times not devoid of a certain effeminate note." The picture entitled *Artemis,* property of the Prado Museum, is attractive in its evocative colouring and the pleasant and expressive naturalness of the female face. Another estimable painter was Francisco Furini who was born in Florence in 1600 and died there in 1646.

The Adoration of the Shepherds by Cavedone.
Prado Museum.

The atmosphere created by Guercino in *Susana and the Old Men* shows the influence of Caravaggio.

Artemis, by Orazio Gentileschi, a painting which highlights the artist's able use of colour.

The greater part of his work is devoted to the female nude. High society in Florence greatly appreciated the languid erotic bodies painted by Furini, all imbued with a light that enhaced to the full the sensual quality of the naked flesh. Furini painted hardly anything but this type of picture until he reached maturity; however, on reaching the age of forty, he apparently underwent a deep spiritual crisis which compelled him to become a priest. From the on the subjetcts of his paintings became radically changed. He stopped painting nudes and devoted himself to exclusively religious themes. Some of his frescoes, such as those on the *Life of St. Lawrence* in the Pitti Palace, are of undoubted quality and reflect the religious feeling that inspired Furini's last artistic phase.

In the Prado is one of the paintings belonging to his initial phase, *Lot and his Daughters,* which evidences Furini's artistic grace in the use of finely muted tones. Andrea Sacchi who was born in Nettuno in 1599 and died in Rome in 1661 was a painter whose work showed a tendency to a classical use of sombre tones. His style was one of a serious attitude to form which was a trifle contrived. The fact that he lived during the flowering of the baroque style nevertheless influenced his classical taste. The overcoming of the rococo and the sprouting of the neoclassical mode in the terrain of art contributed to the enhancing of Sacchi's prestige as a painter among his contemporaries. His best frescoes were those painted in Rome, the best known being *The Vision of St. Romualdo. Portrait of the Painter Francesco Albani* in the Prado is a good example of Andrea Sacchi's excellent gifts as a painter.

Another Italian artist of merit was Salvator Rosa. Born in 1615 on the outskirts of Rome, he died in Rome in 1673.

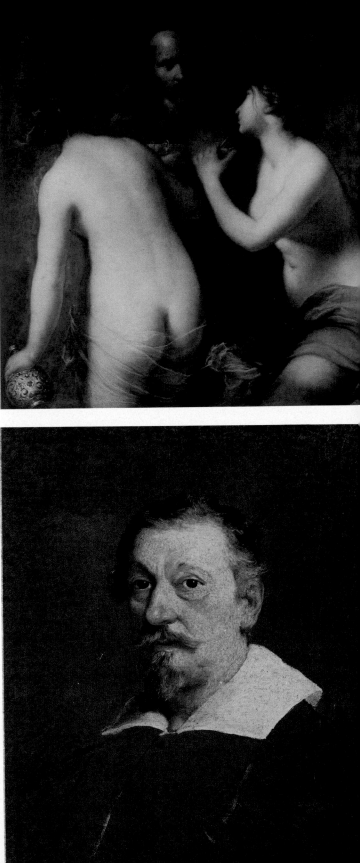

St. Cayetano before the Virgin, the Child, and
St. Joseph by Andrea Vaccaro; *Lot and his daughters*,
by Francesco Furini, and *The Painter Francesco Albani*,
by Andrea Sacchi, all three paintings to be found
in the Prado Museum.

Christ with Saints in Glory, en ambitious painting
by Mattia Preti in the Prado.

The Gulf of Salerno, one of the most characteristic
works by Salvator Rosa, a landscape artist with a
romantic temperament who was able to create unusual
atmospheres in paint and expressed himself in daring
brush strokes using a muted and at the same time
darkened colouring.

Rosa was indeed a man of many sided talent as he was not only a painter but a poet, musician, actor, director of plays and also an excellent public speaker. He was passionately fond of nature and his paintings reveal a vivacious romantic temperament. Perhaps his landscapes are the best of his work. With daring brush strokes and deep colours, Rosa penetratingly captured the rhythm of the landscapes he painted. He also treated historical and military subjects especially the painting of battles. He appeared to enjoy depicting the horror of combat with its wake of slaughter in his pictures. One of his most prized works is the painting entitled *Peace among the Shepherds*. In the Prado Museum there is a work of his *The Gulf of Salerno* in which the artist has poured all his romantic passion for nature.

LUCAS JORDAN

Luca Giordano, as he is known in Italian, was born in Naples in 1632 and died there in 1705. One of the most famous painters of his time, he studied with Ribera and Pedro de Cortona. He possessed a extravert personality and an extraordinary facility — the speed with which he painted earned him the nickname of "Lucas fa presto", or "speedy Luke", but he was lacking in genuinely creative inspiration. "Luca Giordano, said Posse, is the archetype of the vistuoso in art, being devoid of professional integrity:

Self-Portrait, an anonymous copy of Lucas Jordán.

he imitated the styles of Ribera, Veronese, Titian, Tintoretto, Bassano, Raphael, Guido Reni and even Dürer, Rembrandt and Rubens, until he merely made forgeries". Giordano lived in Naples, Rome, Florence, Venice, Bergamo and Genoa, receiving a warm welcome everywhere. He was showered with honours by the Pope and stayed in Spain as court painter from 1692 to 1702. During this time he decorated some royal rooms for Charles II and the domes of El Escorial, the Palacio Real, the Buen Retiro, the church of Atocha (Madrid) and the cathedral of Toledo. Giordano's painting tends to be spectacular. He is shallow and tends to a manierist appearance. He painted on several biblical, mythological and historical subjects, and there are also some still life studies and portraits painted by Giordano. He was extremely prolific and it is calculated that he painted some 5,000 pictures throughout his lifetime, but his work is not of much interest to the modern critic.

He is represented in the Prado Museum by an equestrian portrait of Charles II and the canvas, *The Battle of San Quintin.*

In his *Portrait of Charles II,* Lucas Jordán reveals his great agility as a painter which was perhaps his main characteristic.

In *The Battle of St. Quintin* by Lucas Jordán, the dynamic nature of the foreground is dramatically though rather theatrically heightened by a circle of lowering black clouds.

Christ served by the Angels, an evocative painting by Alexandro Magnasco in the Prado Museum.

An excellent *Self-Portrait* by Francesco Solimena on show in the Prado Museum.

MAGNASCO

This painter from Genoa (1667-1749) enjoyed much prestige among his contemporaries. Fond of painting pictures of small dimensions, he showed great ability in depicting scenes from daily life. He succeeded in painting a true reflection of the most diverse popular types: gypsies, amateur singers, soldiers, comedians, nuns, craftsmen etc. His painting is attractive in its anecdotic appeal. Alexandro Magnasco gave a vivacious quality to everything he painted. During these last centuries critics have not treated him so well, usually accusing him of being imitative and rather shallow. However, Magnasco is worthily represented in the Prado Museum by a painting entitled, *Christ served by the Angels,* a pleasant work showing artistic flexibility and an element of fantasy.

SOLIMENA

Francesco Soliman (1657-1747), known in the art world by the name of Solimena, was essentially a painter in the decorative baroque style. He lived most of his life in Naples and it was there where he painted practically all his pictures. He was an extremely facile artist showing a complete mastery of his profession. He even said he was capable of painting in a dozen different styles. And it is this very facility from which his work suffers as he has no special preference for any subject. It was the same for him to paint a portrait as to decorate walls in the most capricious manner. He was, nevertheless, an undoubtedly talented artist who was probably unable to do justice to his great gifts. He was the head of a school of art.

AMICONI

Jacopo Amiconi was born in Venice in 1675 and died in Madrid in 1752. He was a painter who travelled extensively throughout Europe. Nevertheless his constant journeying did not stop him from producing many works of art. He was much appreciated during his lifetime and his painting highly esteemed by his contemporaries. But after his death this painter became completely forgotten.

Amiconi spent several years in the service of the Elector of Bavaria as his official painter, being commissioned to paint a large number of allegorical compositions in different palaces, along with works of a religious nature for different churches in Bavaria. Later on he went to London where he also lived for some time. There, he gained entrée into aristocratic circles and did many portraits of nobles and outstanding people of the time. An inveterate traveller, Amiconi was unable to settle anywhere. When he became tired of one city, he sought to go to another. He also lived in Paris where once again he became known as a facile and elegant painter. The same can be said of his stay in Spain.

Jacopo Amiconi was a characteristic representative of the rococo style. His painting was gay and decorative but lacking in profundity. He was too facile an artist and his work looks rather frivolous from a present day standpoint. He is considered to be a precursor of Tiepolo. There are two paintings of his in the Prado, *El Marqués de la Ensenada,* and *The Infanta Maria Teresa Antonia,* both of which faithfully reflect his style.

Jacopo Amiconi reveals his ability as a portrait painter in this work entitled *The Marquis de la Ensenada*.

The *Infanta María Teresa Antonia*, another of the portraits by Amiconi in the Prado.

TIEPOLO

Giovanni Battista Tiepolo, born in Venice in 1696 and died in 1770 in Madrid, was one of the last great painters of the Venetian school, the other being Guardi. Tiepolo's powerful personality filled the period from the development of baroque to rococo. A member of a wealthy family, he began his apprenticeship as an artist with Gregorio Lazzarini. Veronese's influence was to be decisive in his work as he was, for Tiepolo, a great source of inspiration; his technique was acquired from Piazzeta. His painting is full of grace and light but perhaps lacking in true vigour.

In 1751 he was summoned to Würzburg where he executed some splendid frescoes in the episcopal residence. These paintings catapulted him to fame. Later, in 1762, he went to Spain at the invitation of King Charles III and painted several frescoes on the domes of the Royal Palace. He also did a large number of frescoes in his native city. Among Tiepolo's oil paintings the most outstanding are, *Telemachus, The Adoration of the Kings, Jesus bearing the Cross* and *The Martyrdom of St. Agatha.* Tiepolo was one of the most celebrated painters of his time. He had an early, somewhat easy triumph. "He was no more than sixteen, says Paul-Jean Mariette, "when he began to draw. He then produced compositions which shone with the fertility of his genius, but it is true that his excessive facility was to his detriment and he could be reproached with being careless and too fond of giving free rein to his imagination. He was not too careful in the verisimilitude of his colours which were false in spite of being attractive. He was never able to draw heads well..."

These criticisms are justified. The work of Tiepolo pleases more by its visual flattery than by its strength and depth. But, however, his creative genius must be respected as it was vastly superior to the artistic capabilities of the majority of the painters of that period. It must not be forgotten that, as Claire Gay states, "it fell to G.B. Tiepolo's lot to lead the new baroque to full autonomy. Early in the century, the fame of this great admirer of Veronese provoked envy. The most flattering commissions for religious and secular decoration constituted the beginning of his overflowing activity. Venice, Germany, and Spain were the main beneficiaries of an art which owed its inspiration and atmosphere to the theatre. Wasn't all the aristocratic life of the period, after all, a kind of play. Tiepolo orchestrated allegory, religion, history, and mythology with the same elegance into a gigantic *ballet* performance, gallant and profane in the extreme. Lovely tumults of bodies came together and dispersed in the infinite space of ceilings painted in light colours. A crowd of curious people, portrayed as in life, lean over balustrades that run along the

An evocative *Head of a Young Girl* by Tiepolo.

cornices. The baroque style was lit up with a smile. In the impetus of this aero *ballet,* bare legs move under the red and yellow shimmer of a swirl of vestments showing up in contrast against the adjacent colder tones. Trumpets melt into clouds infused with light. Bodies appear in the dizzy foreshortening of ascending movement. It is impossible to enter into the details of a work which from the Rezzonico, Clerici or Canossa palaces, to the villas of the Contarini, Soderini, or Cordellina, covered the walls of patrician houses with delirious allegory. Rarely had decorative painting assumed such different aspects. The motly crowd from

Tiepolo was an able painter of religious subjects as this canvas of his entitled *The Immaculate Conception* reveals.

forth mythology and carnivals in the seven rooms of the house where *chinoiseries* and *fêtes galantes* of a surprisingly natural quality are to be found". This is so; Claire Gay is right in that the baroque style found in Tiepolo "the dimension it needed for its splendour". There are several of Tiepolo's works in the Prado, among them, *Abraham and the three Angels,* a real prodigy of artificial grace—, *St. Antonio de padua with the Child Jesus, Angel bearing the Eucharist,* and *Head of a Young Girl.*

Abraham and the Three Angels, one of the best of the paintings by Tiepolo on show in the Prado Museum.

the carnival bursts into the Papadopoli palace with masks, charlatans and musicians. The frescoes in the Labia palace tell of the tragic love of Mark Anthony and Cleopatra, and the palace becomes a theatre.

But perhaps it is the villa Valmarana which contains the most diverse aspects, a constantly renewed fantasy from baroque to rococo. In this palace, tribute is paid to the theatre in the great salon with the *Sacrifice of Iphigenia.* The epic poetry of Virgil, Homer, Ariosto and Tasso provided the gallant subject matter for the decoration of the four consecutive rooms; and a dazzling inspiration brought

St. Anthony of Padua with the Child Jesus and Angel bearing the Eucharist, both works by Tiepolo in the Prado Museum.

The Battle at Clavijo, one of the paintings by Giaquinto in the Prado Museum.

In The Birth of the Sun and the triumph of Bacchus, Giaquinto demonstrates his fondness for grandiloquence in painting.

Two
landscapes
characteristic
of Joli: *The
Embarcation
of Charles III
at Naples;*
two variations
on the same
theme.

The Birth and Childhood of Christ, a magnificent triptych by an unknown Flemish artist.

THE FLEMISH SCHOOL

This school is fairly well represented in the Prado Museum. In the XIV and XV centuries there was already a very important and flourishing artistic tradition in Flanders, with a constellation of outstanding painters—Jan Van Eyck, Roger constellation of oustanding painters—Jan Van Eyck, Roger Vam der Weyden, Maestro de Flemalle, Gerard David, Memling, Metsys, Joachim de Patinir—filling the commercial cities with pictures with a delicate sensitivity which are today still full of enchantment and are prized examples. All of these were created by artists of an even temperament who carried out their task heedless of time, with patience and care. There is something of the craftsman in their compositions, the Middle Ages are ever present in their work, with their ordered sense of life and unbending religiosity. There is also a certain aristocratic distance to be observed in these Flemish paintings. Nevertheless, the revolution of the Renaissance was developing with its subsequently strong influence on artistic production. Hypolite Taine refered in his *Philosophie de l'Art,* to the end of the Middle Ages in the Low Countries, saying that "their art is not similar to that of Italy as each springs from different cultural and spiritual tendencies. One realizes this on reading the ingenuous, vulgar verses recited by the church and the Virtues: coarse clumsy poetry, verbiage of mediocre minstrels, strings of rhyming phrases with a rhythm as weak as their content. Then there was no Dante, Petrarch, Bocaccio or Villani. Their spirit, less precocious and farther from the latin tradition was held for longer in the inert grip of the Middle Ages. Faith and Christian feeling are stronger and more tenacious in this part of the world than in Venice of Florence: they merely subsist under the sensual pomp of the court at Bologna. If there exist epicures in customs, they do not exist in theory; the most gallant serve religion as they do ladies in matters of honour. On the other hand, architecture, which among the arts is what best expresses the necessity of popular imagination, continued to be Gothic and Christian until the middle of the XVI century, and was not affected by Italian and Classical influences; its style became complicated and feminine but did not change. This didn't only appertain in ecclesiastical but also in secular building; in Bruges, Louvain, Brussels, Liège and Oudenard, the town hall buildings show to what extent their style was approved by both the clergy and the nation as a whole. " Flemish painting of the XIV, XV and even XVI centuries was similarly affected.

MAESTRO DE FLEMALLE
ROBERT CAMPIN, VAN EYCK

The XV century painter generally considered, along with Van Eyck, to be one of the founders of the Flemish school is thought by some authors to be Robert Campin. Maestro de Flemalle lived in the XV century and apparently worked in Brugues, Liège, and Tournai, and also in some towns in the north of France. "Critics, wrote Michel Hérubel, have considered works such as *The Virgin on the Throne* in the museum at Aix-en-Provence, *the altar piece shutter,* a bequest of Hemrich von Werl, *The Virgin of the osier lamp shade* and a *Nativity,* to belong to Maestro de Flemalle, these works are painted in cold colours but their landscapes are a forestate of Brueghel. In spite of all this, there is, in Flemalle's work a lack of density which makes us doubt." In the Prado there is a *St. Barbara* attributed to Maestro Flemalle. There are though, those who claim it was really painted by Van der Weyden.

Robert Campin was probably born around 1375; what is certain is that he was living in Tournai in 1406 and died in 1444. Campin had an important studio in Tournai which at that time was under French domination, and it was there where he painted the many commissions he received. Rogier Van der Weyden and Jacques Daret were pupils of his. Robert Campin's works are unknown and certain authors attribute to him those painted by Maestro Flemalle. Jan Van Eyck was born between 1390 and 1400 on the banks of the Meuse in the locality which bears his name, and died in Bruges on July 8th 1441. One of his brothers, Hubert (1366-1426) collaborated with him in several of his works. Jan Van Eyck decorated the palace of the Hague in 1422 (the paintings being no longer extant), and three years later he became the painter and gentleman in waiting to Philip the Goold, duke of Burgundy. Among his most famous paintings are those entitled *The Madonna and the Chancellor Rolin,* an extraordinarily beautiful painting, now kept in the Louvre, *The Madonna and the Ecclesiastic van der Paele, Portrait of Arnolfini, the Altarpiece of the Lamb of God, The Madonna in the cathedral, The Virigin of Lucca* and *The Man in a Turban.*

Van Eyck's painting is eminently serene and peaceful. He was the first to resolve the technical problems of depicting movement, perspective, colour and proportion in details in a convincing manner. In the work of the founder of the Flemish school, all these problems appear to be effectively resolved. His world is essentially one of a deep feeling of order and balance. "Jan van Eyck is a prodigious realist, said Hérubel, for the fist time in painting he made his subject converse with the spectator. In his famous picture

St. Barbara, a Flemish painting attributed to Maestro de Flemalle.

Man in a Turban, the gaze of the subject is fixed on us and conveys a message of intense inner life. Perhaps this painting is his self-portrait, we would like to believe this to be so, as it would be the only painting to represent its author. Here there is revealed at the same time, all that XV century man had of the Middle Ages in his attitude and all that can be expressed in the eyes of a forerunner of humanism.

There is, in the Prado, an excellent example of Jan van Eyck's style and his mastery of technique — *The Fountain of Grace and the Triumph of the Church over the Synagogue.* Of special note is the precision with which the finest details are executed and the balance of the work as a whole.

Obverse of the work entitled *Betrothal of the Virgin* by Robert Campin.

The Fountain of Grace and the triumph of the Church over the Synagogue, a painting by Van Eyck in the Prado Museum, in which the style and technique characteristic of the works of this famous Flemish primitive are clearly observed.

VAN DER WEYDEN

The Van de Weyden family made up a dynasty in Flemish painting, they were Rogier, Peter, and Goswyn, the two latter being respectively the son and grandson of the former. Rogier van der Weyden, the most important painter of the three was born in 1399 in Tournai and died in Brussels in 1464. He was also known by the name of Roger de la Pasture. Little is known of his personality and his life. "There is no document, says Erik Larsen, which allows us to identify any of the works usually attributed to him with certainty. He never signed a painting; and the scanty data found in the archives only succeed in confusing an already confused situation".

Van der Weyden was a pupil of Robert Campin and a fellow pupil of Jacques Daret. After Van Eyck, he was the painter who most influenced Flemish art. In 1436, he was appointed official painter of the city of Brussels. In Italy he studied the works of the Italian masters, mainly in Rome and Ferrara. "Roger van der Weyden, says Michel Hérubel, is a painter of grace. Less inspired than van Eyck in the domain of the quasi supernatural, more humane than Memling, although his style during his mature period tended towards the spiritual–, he vas able to fuse the human and the divine in hist art. His work produces a sense of balance, so much so that he could almost pass for a French artist: he is a Roger van der Weyden is excellent. His drawing with its delicate lines, richness of colour, the gracefulness of his characters and at the same time the authority of their gestures, even more accentuated by the simplicity and the evocation of peace which they imply, all constitute the incomparable style of the master of Tournai."

The Virgin and Child by Van der Weyden is one of the most admired paintings from the Flemish school in the Prado Museum; the drawing is perfect, the figures highly expressive, and the use of colour particularly luminous, dominated by the bright red of the Virgin's dress.

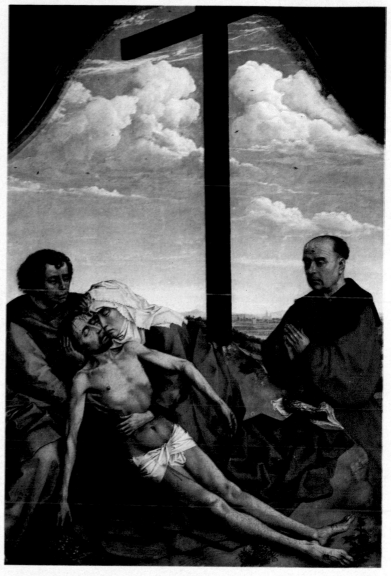

Piety, by Van der Weyden, a harmoniously balanced work in colour and in composition.

Among the most famous works by Van der Weyden are:
*The Angelic Salutation, The Triptych of the Redemption,
Triptych of the Braque Family, Piety, The Crucifixion, Triptych of the seven Sacraments, Portrait of Philip de Croy,
Portrait of Antonio, the Great Bastard of Burgundy, Portrait of Francesco d'Este,* and *The Last Judgement.* His
painting is anointed with a Gothic-like' grace. His nudes
are ascetic in quality but not devoid at times of human
charm. One of the artist's most important works in the
Prado Museum is the *Descent from the Cross,* a well balanced painting with a rich use of colour. *The Descent* by

Van der Weyden, says Eugenio D'Ors, appears before us
like a triumphal gateway at the en trance to Flemish painting: Van der Weyden went to Rome and it is said that
he was the first Flemish artist whose merit was recognised
by the Italians. He is certainly the painter who best
retained the classical sense among all his compatriots. His
works are very close to scuplture having in common with
Poussin and Mantegna, something of painted bas reliefs.
Other interesting works by the same author in the Prado
Museum are *The Virgin and Child, Piety, Redemption,* and
The Crucifixión.

The Visitation, one of Bouts' most characteristic paintings of those in the Prado Museum.

The Annunciation, another work by Bouts on show in the Prado Museum.

BOUTS

Born around the year 1400 in Haarlem, Dierck Bouts died in 1475. He was the official painter for the city of Louvain where he was twice married, being 70 years of age on the second occasion. Bouts was one of the artists who most influenced Dutch painting and that of the Lower Rhine. A skilful draughtsman, he had a complete mastery of technique. Perhaps he did not have a very strong creative imagination, but his talent excelled tremendously when it came to reflecting expression on the human face. He was also a painter who had great ability with landscapes as can be observed by examining the background in many of his pain-

tings. Another characteristic of this Dutch painter is the formal elegance of all his compositions. Among his most famous works, mention must be made of, *The Martyrdom of St. Erasmus, The Holy Sacrament,* whose altar piece is considered his masterpiece, *The Iniquitous Sentence of the Emperor Oton, Reparation for the Injustice he Committed, Portrait of Man, Virgin with Child,* and *The Adoration of the Magi.* Refering to the first of the aforementioned works, Michel Hérubel wrote: "Bouts has been criticised for a certain phlegmatic quality in his minutely detailed depiction of torture and a coldness in his treatment of subject matter. (This criticism was also made of his *Martyrdom of St. Hippolytus* in Bruges.) St. Erasmus is lying tied to a

The Adoration of the Angels, by Dierck Bouts.

The Adoration of the Magi, by Bouts.

board half naked. His stomach has been perforated and a winch has been fixed to the ends of his intestines worked by two executioners, a bald old man with bare arms and a frightening appearance who is vigorously turning the handle, and a young man, not very accustomed to the business, and more or less charitable in appearance. A bearded person – a type often seen with some variations in different paintings by this artist in, for example, the doors of *The Supper* –, a finely dressed person in authority wearing garments of blue and gold brocade lined with fur, is leaning on a rod of office and watching the victim and his executioners with dignity and simplicity, as if passively complying with an official formality; his three helpers, among them the one on the left, probably an Arian priest, observe the spectacle or avert their gaze from it in an uninterested fashion. Behind this group is a verdant landscape furrowed with roads and full of hills with those at Kessel and Lo-obergen not far from Louvain being easily recognisable. Was Bouts an apathetic, distant painter as we have heard say? We don't think so. The fact is he had a style very much his own, and despite this appearance of coldness and even at times of brusqueness, we find an enormous sensitivity in his painting".

There are several works by Bouts in the Prado – *The Visitation, The Annunciation, The Adoration of the Angel,* and *The Adoration of the Kings.*

MEMLING

Hans Memling was of German origin, born in Memlingen, a town near Mentz, between 1435 and 1440. He died in Bruges in 1494 and was apparently a pupil of Rogier Van der Weyden. Memling, or more correctly, Memlinc, built up the Bruges school of painting which before his time had gone through a period of decadence. He was one of the best portrait painters of his time. His pictures being almost all half length. He was prolific, and few are the museums of note that do not possess one of his works. Among his best known portraits are those entitled, *Man with a Medal,* kept in Antwerp, *Martin van Nieuwenhove,* now in Bruges, and *A Young Man,* now in New York. Memling was also an expert on religious paintings. The faces of his Virgins produce a deep sensation of sweetness. Almost all his work of a religious nature was impregnated with restfulness and peace. Significant of this phase is *The Virgin among the Saints,* one of his best works, now in Bruges. Sometimes, very occasionally, a touch of drama is introduced into these religious paintings as, for example, in his *Descent from The Cross.* But this is not the predominating note; rather is it that of a serenely sweet inner balance.

Fierens-Gevaert makes the following judgement on Memling: "This great Flemish ecclectic has assimilated into his genius the technique of Jan Van Eyck, the lyricism of Rogier van der Weyden, the religiosity of Bouts, the facial observations of Van der Goes, and the brilliant analytical quality of the miniaturists". Several critics are reticent about the work of this Flemish painter. "Memlinc, says Hérubel, has also been accused of being insipid. Some critics have even reproached him for being affected. This is unjust. Memlinc expressed above all sweetness; he had a subtle lyricism, and was one of the painters who knew how to evoke in a penetrating way the ideal of peace on earth, the peace that prepares human beings for the peace of God. Seen in this way, Memlinc is still a completely mediaeval artist. His paintings exemplify the great delicacy of his feeling, together with a deep psychological study of the human face".

There are many works by Hans Memling in Spain. In the art collection in the Royal Chapel at Granada, where paintings by Van der Weyden, Bouts and Hieronymus Bosch are also kept, there are two fine pictures by Memling: *The Holy Women* and *The Descent.* In the Prado he is represented by several works of great quality: *Virgin and Child among the Angels* — of an evocative and delicate beauty, *The Adoration of the Magi, Nativity, Purification —,* all of them highly representative of the artist's style.

A unique sweetness emanates from this lovely work by Memling *The Virgin among the Angels;* here the artist has expressed all his poetic sensitivity in paint.

The Adoration of the Magi, Nativity, and *The Purification* are three paintings by Hans Memling in the Prado Museum.

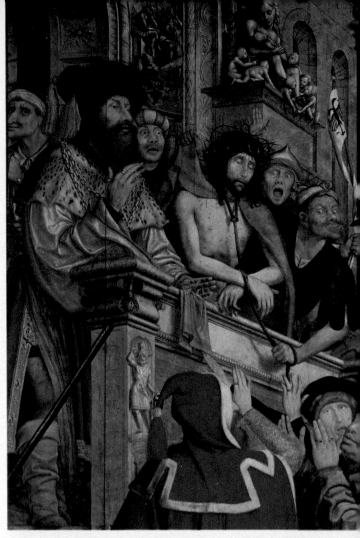

Rest during the flight into Egypt, by Gerard David

Christ before the People and *Old Woman tearing her hair,* both paintings are by Quentin Metsys.

GERARD DAVID

Born in 1450 in Oudewater (Utrecht), this Dutch painter who died in Bruges in 1523, remained forgotten for three long centuries. His name was saved from oblivion in 1866 when some records were discovered in Bruges that contained diverse documents related to him.

Gerard David learned to paint in Haarlem and later, between 1470 and 1480, he lived in Italy which explains the marked Italian-rooted Renaissance influence to be observed in most of his work. In 1483, David became a member of the Guild of St. Luke in Bruges. He was commissioned by the Town Hall of Bruges to paint two pictures alluding to Law and Justice which were finished in 1498. It is easy to see the influence of the Florentine school in both these paintings. Gerard David's masterpiece is the altar piece *Jean des Trompes* in which we are attracted by the carefully depicted landscape. David's painting in the Prado is a fine one entitled *Virgin and Child.*

The Virgin of Louvain, another work by Mabuse in the Prado Museum

METSYS

This artist, along with Memling and Gerard David formed the great trilogy of the Bruges school of painting. Quentin Metsys (1466-1530) was the son of a blacksmith, a trade the future painter learned and to which he apparently intended to devote himself; this however did not transpire as he not to know the daughter of the painter Van Tuylt and fell in love with her. This, at least, is what is traditionally related. He appears to have been in Germany and England and to have learnt painting in these countries. Having demonstrated his qualities as an artist, he married the daughter of Van Tuylt and became one of the most successful Flemish painters of his time. Among his best known works are, *The Burial of Christ,* in Antwerp museum and *The Banker and his Wife* in the Louvre.

Virgin with the Child, a painting by Jan Gossart Mabuse (1478-1533) in which it is not difficult to observe the influence of Dürer.

MABUSE

Han Gossaert Mabuse was born in the village whose name he bore (in Flemish, Maubuege), around 1478, and died in Middelburg in Holland between 1533 and 1536. He spent some time in Italy with the entourage of Philip of Burgundy and certain authors claim he was the artist who introduced a fondness for nudes and their portrayal into Flemish painting. In some of the works of Mabuse, *The Virgin and Child,* for example, now in the Prado, there is a certain tendency to a depiction of the human body in a style not exactly distinguished by its naturalness. In Mabuse's nudes there is a tendency to a sculptural expression as well as a pictorical one in that volumes are seen to be important. In his work, purely sculptural values are of greater moment than colour, light, and even the reflection of an inner world through the expression on human faces. Mabuse was a master of the technique of portrait painting. One of his best works being the *Portrait of Jean de Carondolet,* now in the Louvre. In his paintings of the Virgin he clearly evidences an emphasis on the sculptural aspect as for example in *Virgin and Child* and *The Virgin of Louvain,* both in the Prado Museum.

The Temptations of St. Anthony is considered the most successful of the three paintings by Patinir in the Prado Museum.

PATINIR

Born around the year 1475 in Bouvignes, a Belgian town near to Dinant, Joaquim Patinir died in 1524 in Antwerp. He was master of the corporation of Antwerp in 1515 and a friend of Quinten Massys, Joos van Cleve and Dürer for whom he was an excellent landscape artist. Little is known of Patinir's life. As an artist he was a tenacious researcher into new dream-like plastic worlds. He, more than any other Flemish artist, used landscape as subjects to be painted in their own right. His landscapes, impregnated with an almost mysterious religiosity, are highly evocative. Another of Patinir's discoveries was the way of solving in paint the problem of aerial perspective. His technique in this consisted of dividing the canvas into three dimensions: the first in a dark colour, the second or intervening plane in green, and the third or background in blue. In all Patinir's work there is still a background of mysticism, strongly redolent of the Middle Ages.

There are three paintings which are highly representative of Patinir's work in the Prado: *The Temptations of San Antonio Abad, The Walk on the Stygian Lake,* and *Rest during the Flight from Egypt.* The first of these depicts St. Antonio Abad trembling, while flashes of lightening fall from the sky and the landscape has a predominant rôle in the composition.

In his works
*The Walk on
the Stygian
Lake* and *Rest
during the Flight
into Egypt*,
all the clarity
and intensity
of Joaquim
Patinir's
particular
aesthetic is
faithfully
reflected.

The excellent artistic qualities
of Barend van Orley are
reflected in his magnificent
picture *The Holy Family* and
also in his *Virgin of the Milk*
both in the Prado Museum.

VAN ORLEY

Barend or Bernart van Orley was born in Brussels in 1492 and died in the same city in 1542. Orley's work includes the new pictorial influences prevalent in the XVI century. Gothic had already been rejected as a pictorial means of communication. Van Orley's paintings already enter into the new manner of the precursors of the Renaissance in Italy. It has not been possible to prove that this painter from Brussels ever went to Italy, but in the majority of his works though not all, the influence of Italian schools can be observed.

Van Orley was an excellent portrait painter. During his stay in the court of Maria of Austria he painted many works of this type. Towards the end of his life he decorated many stained glass windows and did designs for tapestries. His *Holy Family,* a truly fine painting, and *The Virgin of the Milk* are both in the Prado Museum.

This *Virgin and Child*
is by the Flemish
artist Jan Sanders
van Hemesen
(1500-1575) who
was born in Hemixen
not far from Antwerp,
and died in Harlem.

The Virgin of the Milk
by Van Orley.

The Surgeon, a curious
work by Hemesen.

The Adoration of the Magi, by Coecke Van Aelst.

Rest during the Flight into Egypt, by Coffermans.

Brueghel the Elder demonstrates his excellence as an artist in his masterpiece *The Triumph of Death*.

BRUEGHEL

There are two Brueghels: Pieter—the Elder, the Rustic, the Rogue, born about 1528 in Brueghel, who died in Brussels in 1569, and Jan—Brueghel de Velours, Brueghel of Paradise, born in Brussels in 1568 who died in 1625 in Antwerp. Both occupy key positions in the history of universal painting. Also painters were Pieter II—Brueghel of Hell, and Pieter III.

Pieter Brueghel was the apprentice of Pieter Coeck, an atist who had travelled widely in Italy and the near East. From him he learnt the secrets of Italian technique. Later he went to the studio of Hieronymus Cock, an engraver and publisher of engravings for whom he did a few copies of Hieronymus Bosch, a painter who exerted great influence over Brueghel the Elder. He also travelled frequently, as his first master did and went to Rome in 1553. Apparently it was in Italy where he stayed for a time and painted his *Naval Battle opposite the Strait of Messina*. Later on he was in collaboration with Cock in his engraving studio and in 1563 married Maria Coeck, the daughter of his first teacher.

Pieter Brueghel devoted himself to painting rather late in life. In 1558 he painted *The Proverbs* and subsequently his most famous works: *Tower of Babel, The Fall of Icarus, Triumph of Death, Fall of the Rebel Angels, Dulle Griet, Preaching of St. John, The Fall of Saul, Hunters in the snow, Fools Paradise, The Beggers* and *Parable*. There is a humourous vein in the pictorical work of Brueghel the Elder in his pictures on social customs, and also a sort of denunciation of injustice and a social protest unknown at the time. "Nature, said Van Mander, made a singularly happy choice the day it selected from among the labourers in an obscure village of Brabant, the humorous Pieter Brueghel, to make him the painter of the peasantry".

Brueghel is one of the most characteristic painters of the Flemish school. He developed his own technique, based of course on that of Hieronymus Bosch for whom he felt the greatest admiration in the field of creative art. Nevertheless, everything in Brueghel appears transformed and enriched by an unusual sensitivity and character. He had a strong creative force and his ability to narrate, always firmly based on reality, and charmingly festive, was surrounded by engagingly original characters. "Of course, said Elie-Charles Flamand, Brueghel had found in the painters of the Low Countries previous to him the subjects, expression and technique, but what makes him admirable is that he was able to broaden certain tendencies and with them create a style without becoming fossilized in conventionality. Moreover, from his stay in Italy, he returned, not with scholastic regulations but with a broadened vision and a stylization which helped him to keep in contact with life. A true humanist, he knew how to share the misfortunes of the peasants of Brabant and to express in his works elevated philosophical concepts which made his friend Ortelius say that "in all his works there is always more thought than painting". With a prodigious clarity, he was conscious of the power and the variety of cosmic forces. Brueghel put the finishing touches to the synthesis of nature and the human soul. If he adapted to realism as much as he did to fantasy, it was because for

him it was only a question of two complementary facets of the ultimate truth. Brueghel was a master of this dialectic of the visible and the invisible, which is one of the more profound aspects of the Neo-Platonic metaphysics of the Renaissance."

Eugenio D'Ors said that, "the path of Hieronymus Bosch is that of humour; the path of Brueghel that of social customs, and the path of Patinir the cult of the landscape". This is a rather rigid and over simplified evaluation. There is something more than humour in Hieronymus Bosch and of course, much more in Brueghel than a mere painter of customs. He has many varied and important qualities all of which are to be found in his artistic creations.

The Triumph of Death, a worthy addition to the Prado collection, in one of the most famous and outstanding works by Brueghel. This is a truly astounding painting of great inspiration. The composition of the picture forms a macabre whole: the legions of Death conquer those of life. Death comes by fire, the scythe or by iron. There are further interesting works by Brueghel in the Prado: the series *The Bodily Senses.* The most outstanding feature of the work of Brueghel the Younger are snow-covered landscapes.

Sight, one of the paintings by Brueghel making up the series entitled *The Bodily Senses*.

Taste, *Touch* and *Hearing*, by Brueghel, part of his series on *The Bodily Senses* in which this great Flemish painter aimed to describe symbolically in paint the life of the senses in the human being.

These two snow covered landscapes both entitled *Snow Scene* represent the work of Brueghel the Younger in the Prado Museum.

POURBUS AND VRANC

There were three painters in the Pourbus family: Peter, born in Gouda (Flanders), about 1510 who died in Bruges in 1584 Franz, Pourbus the Elder, son of Pieter, born in 1545 in Bruges who died in Amsterdam in 1581, and the son of the latter, Franz Pourbus the Younger, who was born in Antwerp in 1569 and died in 1622 in Paris.

Franz Pourbus the Elder was a pupil of Franz Floris whose daughter he married in 1569. Later, in 1578 he was married again to Anna Mahieu. Among his most important works is his *Christ among the Doctors*, kept in the church of San Bavon, Ghent. Like his father, he was an able portrait painter, and other interesting works of his are: *Viglius Ayta, The Wedding of the Painter Hoefnaegel, Gilles de Schmidt,* and *Portrait of Juan de Hambyse.*

Franz Pourbus the Younger went to Italy where he was court painter in Mantua from 1600 to 1609. In Paris he carried out the same function in the court of the Queen Mother Mary de Medici where he was apparently introduced through the good offices of Rubens. An excellent portrait painter, many influences are apparent in his work, among them the Spanish. Actually, he was a rootless cosmopolitan and produced uneven work. He was fond of depicting life-sized human figures. In the Prado Museum is his *Portrait of Isabel of France, wife of Philip IV.*

Sebastian Vranc who was born in Antwerp in 1573 and died there in 1647 was a person with an outstanding social personality. He occupied the position of President of the Corporation of St. Luke, was Dean of the Rhetorical Association and captain of the civic guard. He spent some time in Italy and specialized in painting battles, assaults by bandits, street brawls and country scenes. There is a painting of his entitled *Siege of Ostend* in the Prado gallery.

Portrait of Isabel of France, wife of Philip IV, painted by Frans Pourbus.

The Siege of Ostende, one of the most characteristic works by Sebastián Vranc.

In *The Adoration of the Magi,* in spite of the rather contrived theme, Rubens is able to reveal all his baroque sensibility.

RUBENS

Although he was born in the German city of Siegen, Westphalia, on June 28th 1577, Peter Paul Rubens (who died in Antwerp in 1640) was a genuinely Flemish painter, not only in the root of his splendid baroque painting but in his own family origin. Rubens was actually born in exile. His father, Johann, an alderman of Antwerp, and a cultured and independent-spirited man, had difficulties with the Spaniards and was obliged to flee from Flanders and settle in Cologne. When this occurred the painter's father had already married Maria Mupelinck, a sweet natured woman with a delicate sensibility who was to be a positive influence on the formation of the future painter of *The Judgement of Paris.*

Rubens began his apprenticeship as a painter with Verghaet. He lived two years with his first master and discovered with pleasure the world to which his vocation was inclined. Later this vocation was to become his whole reason for living. From Verghaet's studio he went to Van Noorth's where he stayed for four years. Then he went to the studio of Otto Voenius, who at that time was the most fashionable

artist in Antwerp. Rubens set out on his first journey in May 1600 and settled for some time in Venice where he was favourably received by the duke of Mantua, Vicente Gonzaga, and was inspired by the vital swagger of this Renaissance personage with his effervescent Dionysiac temperament which probably proved fruitful for the painter. In all Rubens' work there is an ever present note, which is more or less accentuated of intense playfulness and spontaneous epicureanism. Accompanied by the duke whose sister in law Maria de Medici was to be married to Henry IV of France, he journeyed to Florence. Later, Vicente Gonzaga commissioned the painter to take to Madrid to the Spanish sovereign and

St. George fighting the Dragon, The Duke of Lerma, Philip II on horseback, and *The Cardinal-Infante Don Fernando of Austria at the battle of Nordlingen* are still more examples of Rubens' vigorous baroque style painting.

The Judgement of Paris, a work of great inspiration and perhaps the grandiose swan song of Rubens' work. The pearly feminine flesh shines in glorious nudity reflecting Rubens' genius in paint. This canvas is one of the finest artistic achievements in the baroque style.

Diana and Calixtus, another inspired painting by Rubens.

In *Andromeda freed by Perseus*, Rubens passionate inspiration creates a sensual mythological work.

The Three Graces by Rubens constitutes an apotheosis in paint of the female nude.

the duke of Lerma, a rich set of jewels and works of art. Rubens also went to Rome where he was warmly received by the Pope and made contact with important personalities there. Rubens was not one of these artists who neglect matters regarding the practical side of life. Quite the contrary; throughout his life he showed that he was as good a painter as he was consummate politician and diplomat. He did not wait for fame to come and honour him, but took definite steps and undertook any negotiations necessary to obtain all kinds of honours. Thus, he did not hesitate in seeking the support of the President of the Supreme Council of Flanders in Madrid and Bishop of Segovia to succeed in getting Philip IV to concede him letters of nobility. The king of Spain acceded to his request and the great Flemish painter and experienced diplomat obtained in June 1624 the right to use the title of Gentleman of the Court. Rubens represents the apotheosis of the baroque style in art and was a man so highly representative of his age that he could hardly have escaped its influence. But Rubens is a painter without artifice; all is passion and pleasure in his splendid work. Rafael

Alberti wrote some extraordinarily penetrating verses on his painting.

> *Era del hombre la pasión, la vida.*
> *Era el caballo que se eleva à hombre,*
> *relámpago las crines y los ojos,*
> *rayos de lluvia enamorada...*

A complex person, Rubens was an impassioned artist, in love with painting and feverishly committed to baroque creation which his contacts with Italian art had helped to purify stylistically. "Not in vain, to use the phrase of his colleague Suttermans, "had he kept Titian in his heart, just as women keep there the chosen one of their thoughts". A person of outstanding culture — suffice it to glance at the subject matter of his paintings to realize that he possessed a cultivated mind; he was a painter who had completely mastered his craft and who bore in mind the minutest details of his professional commitment. He was a born painter, gifted with a special predisposition for mastering means of expression in paint. "About ten colours, especially primary colours and

Rubens evidences his dynamic baroque style in his
work *The Rape of Hipodamia*.

complementary ones, said Leo van Puybelde, were sufficient to create the dazzling splendour that strikes us in the work of this most prestigious of painters".

While the painting of Hieronymus Bosch was in a way, like the reflection in paint of that psychic contraction arising from the mediaeval conflict on coming into contact with the Renaissance, Ruben's work is a Dionysiac apotheosis arising from Renaissance serenity clashing with baroque fervour. There are several works by Rubens of undisputed quality on show in the Prado Museum. We will mention two of the most famous: *The Judgement of Paris,* and *Nymphs and Satyrs.* The first is an enormous canvas 199 × 379 painted by Rubens two years before his death. It belongs to the series of paintings commissioned by Philip IV to decorate his

hunting pavilion (Torre Parada). A painting of great inspiration, it is a sort of grandiose swan song within the context of Rubens'art. The pearly female flesh shines in glorious nudity depicted by the sovereign art of this great Flemish master. This canvas is one of the greatest achievements of baroque painting, its composition, execution and use of colour are wisely assembled and the whole forms a true masterpiece of baroque art. The nakedness of the three graces is completely devoid of any taint of obscenity. Everything in these naked forms is a harmonious hymn to liberty and love. Furthermore in *Nymphs and Satyrs* Rubens portrays his baroque style and feeling to the fullest extent and succeeds in depicting a group which breaks with the rigid mythological concepts – a subject entirely made for him.

*Diana and her nymphs
surprised by Fauns,* a
painting by Rubens full of
vigour and agility within the
baroque context.

Saturn devouring a Child, and *The Birth of the Milky Way*, mythological subjects masterfully painted by Rubens in the baroque style.

Rubens, as a painter always appears to take pleasure in the depiction of feminine flesh and achieves some fine effects in the nudes in his work *Nymphs and Satyrs*.

Rest during the Flight into Egypt by Rubens. In this work, the landscape is also immersed in the subtle baroque aura of the painting.

In his *Garden of Love* Rubens projects his well known fondness for the sensual and the luxuriant.

St. Paul, a magnificent work by Rubens among the many by this artist in the Prado Museum.

St. Peter the Apostle is not a typical painting of Rubens'. The characteristically baroque tone of Rubens' work is slightly muted in this picture presumably because of its subject matter.

The Judgement of Solomon, a very typical painting of Rubens.

In *The Wild Boar at Bay* Snyders demonstrates his excellent ability to depict hunting scenes.

The Cook in the Pantry, a fine still life by Snyders.

CRAYER AND DE VOS

Gaspard de Crayer was born in Antwerp in 1584 and died in Ghent in 1669. A friend of Rubens and Van Dyck, he first worked in the court of the Cardinal-Infante in Ghent and was later appointed court painter to the king of Spain. He lived in Madrid until 1664 when he returned to Ghent. Crayer was an able portrait painter as shown in his work entitled *The Infante Don Fernando de Austria dressed as a Cardinal,* now in the Prado Museum.

There were three painters with the surname De Vos: Cornelis, Marten, and Paul.

Cornelis de Vos was born in 1584 in Hulst and died in Antwerp in 1651. After Rubens and Van Dyck he was the most famous portrait painter of his day.

Marten de Vos was born in Antwerp about 1532 and died there in 1603. He was a pupil and assistant of Tintoretto in Venice and worked for the Medici family. On his return to Antwerp he gained considerable success as a portrait painter and painter of religious subjects.

Paul de Vos was the brother of Cornelis. He was born in Amsterdam around 1596 and died there in 1678. This painter specialized in depicting hunting and animal scenes. His pictures, especially those on hunting themes are attractive in their dynamic appeal. His work is rather similar to that of his brother in law Snyders, but has brighter colours although less elegance. His still life pictures are also charming, as well as his compositions of instruments and fire arms. Paul de Vos' aesthetic qualities are admirably reflected in the picture *Stag persued by the Pack* in the Prado Museum.

Portrait of the Infante Don Fernando of Austria dressed as a Cardinal by Jasper de Crayer.

Deer Persued by the Pack by Paul de Vos a painter who specialized in Still Life pictures and hunting themes.

The vigorous artistic sensibility of Jordaens is amply
revealed in his magnificent *Three Musicians.*

JORDAENS

Jacobo Jordaens was born and died in Antwerp (1593-1678), and with Rubens and Van Dyck formed the great three of XVII century Flemish painting. The son of a well to do merchant, he began to study art in the studio of Adam Van Noort whose daughter he married in 1616. He got to know Rubens and apparently painted several pictures which Rubens had been commissioned to paint and had been unable to do. He travelled through Italy and copied several paintings by famous masters. In 1621 he was appointed Dean of the Guild of St. Luke. The King of England commissioned some paintings from him to decorate his castle at Greenwich; these have now disappeared. In spite of having became a Protestant, Jordaens continued to receive commissions from catholic churches.

Jacobo Jordaens was passionately devoted to painting. Intellectual considerations were for him purely incidental. What really interested him were artistic values. He was a temperamental rather than a meditative artist who became inebriated with colour. The sumptuous colouring of his pictures attracted Rubens' admiration and he always held Jordaens in high esteem. Among the paintings belonging to his initial phase, colour is everything, subject matter being for him a mere pretext for painting. His best known works

are: *Satyr visiting a Peasant, Popular Banquets, The Fertility of the Earth, Like Father like Son.* Colour is predominant in all these works, the first an absolute burst of colour, the others slightly more muted. Paintings from his later years, *Moses striking the Rock,* or *Tribute from St. Peter,* evidence a much less sensual use of colour.

Jordaens can be considered a true specialist in the painting of family groups. His pictures of this type: *The Baby King, Portrait of an armed man accompanied by his Parents,* or *Concert,* are outstanding examples of this style. He appeared to be rather less at home in the depiction of religious themes but in spite of this he was able to show his great ability as a painter in several works of this type viz. *The Martyrdom of St. Apolline, St. Carlos Borromeo,* and *Christ on the Cross.*

Jordaens was an epicure and a confirmed sensualist and in this as in other respects, he was very like Rubens. "Jordaens, says Philippe Daudy, was a bourgeois, a strong spirit. He was inclined to the tangible, the concrete, as in Bouvard and Pécuchet, by Flaubert for fear, who knows? of being cheated. The passionate tenderness of Rubens was completely strange to him and the veiled irony of Van Dyck must have irritated him. He knew that only colour was truth, along with his canvas and brushes. The paint itself was a pretext for painting. "Before Rubens, from whom he only took the manner, he was influenced by Bassano and Caravaggio. His

religious paintings: *The Adoration of the Shepherds* and *Triumph of the Eucharist,* are in this sense as convincing or as lacking as his vast free sketches. "If he hadn't been such an able painter Jordaens would perhaps have been one of these great decorators in the style of Le Brun. He lacked the dignity that comes from a sense of authority. Furthermore, he became converted to Protestantism at the end of his life. He had the blindness of the craftsman, linseed oil and turpentine were his ambrosia". These terms used by Daudy appear somewhat exaggerated, but he is partly right. Painting, for Jordaens, was essentially a material thing, tactile and visible. He was a glutton for colour, a lover of life for its own sake and his painting was truly "a hymn to reality" as Daudy put it. There are several excellent works by Jacobo Jordaens in the Prado Museum. D'Ors was captivated by "just one picture, the smallest, which isn't a painting in the classical sense of the word. Spare a glance for *The Three Musicians* so joyfully sketched. Why this particular picture? Because the modernity of Jordaens is revealed here, in the technique more openly than in any other work in the museum including Goya. This is the Prado painting that least deserves to be there."

In effect, this is an unconventional work par excellence; Eugenio D'Ors wanted to express this in his description. Jordaens' art is also well represented in the works entitled *The Jordaens Family in a garden,* and *Meleagro and Atalanta* both in the Prado collection.

The Family of Jordaens, a work in which the Flemish artist reveals his mastery of the art of painting.

Meleagro and Atalanta, a painting by Jordaens in the Prado Museum.

Self-Portrait of Van Dyck to the left of the picture, and *Portrait of Sir Endymion Porter*, a work in which the great qualities of this famous Flemish portrait painter are convincingly revealed.

VAN DYCK

Although he did not live beyond the age of forty two, Anton Van Dyck was one of the artists who made a deep impression on XVII century painting, especially on the Flemish and English schools. Born in Antwerp in 1599, Van Dyck died in his residence at Blackfriars (England) in 1641. He was the son of a rich merchant and received the appropriate education for one of his class. Almost nothing is known about his early years. In 1618, when he was only 19 years old, Van Dyck entered as a master in the painters' guild at Antwerp. At this time he was in close collaboration with Rubens who considered him his best pupil. It was Rubens who first influenced Van Dyck. The two painters were in the service of the aristocracy and in both the mark of the baroque can clearly be seen. But Van Dyck was more measured than Rubens, more intelligent and refined. His character and manners were courteous and distinguished. Around the year 1620, Anton Van Dyck, who had already acquired solid prestige as a portrait painter in his own country, set sail for the first time, for the coast of England, at the invitation of the Earl of Arundel, a famous British collector. Van Dyck worked for three months in the service of James I, then he went to Italy, where he was considerably influenced by Titian in his modern concept of the portrait. He was in Antwerp once again in 1627. Re-

quests for portraits painted by his masterly hand rained on him from all parts. Not only did the rich members of the middle class and high dignitaries of church and court wish to be painted, but also Isabel Clara Eugenia, the then Queen Regent of the Low Countries desired to have her portrait painted by him. He went on a journey to Holland, and after to England once more, where he founded an artists' guild and became its director. This painter from Antwerp enjoyed great prestige and popularity at the English court, and Charles I gave him a title. He did many portraits, including some of the king and his family, charging fabulous sums and leading the life of a potentate.

In 1634 he went on a journey to Flanders and tried to buy a country house on the outskirts of Antwerp, but was not able to do this, the house in question being bought by Rubens. One of Van Dyck's most famous works was painted in 1634, this was the collective portrait (a vast canvas) of the members of the Brussels Municipal Council. A year later he returned to England and settled in London as he had done before, in great luxury. He led a life of constant pleasure having completely adapted to the dissolute atmosphere of the English court, and became a perfect hedonist. He felt highly satisfied with himself, knew he was admired by the king and his courtiers and was well aware that in England he was considered the greatest painter of his contempora-

The Painter Martin Ryckaert, Charles I of England,
and *Diana and Endymion surprised by a Faun,* three
paintings by Van Dyck on show in the Prado
Museum.

ries. He earned enormous sums of money with his work which allowed him to live in great splendour. Charles I himself went to visit him in his studio. The English aristocracy literally fought to have Van Dyck paint their portrait. He also had as many lady friends as he could wish for; today one mistress tomorrow another. He was the spoilt darling of London, and everything became him. But one woman burst in upon Van Dyck's life with a hurricane-like passion. She was Margaret Lemon, one of the painter's mistresses in London. In 1639 Van Dyck had married Mary Ruthwen, granddaughter of the Earl of Gowrie. His dissipated artist's life was not an impediment to his marrying an aristocrat. Conventionally, all the English aristocrats did the same; they enjoyed their pleasures as long as age allowed and then they made an honest marriage to a high-born virtuous young woman. But it was then when something happened that Van Dyck was probably very far from expecting and which must have greatly perturbed his delicate sensibility. Margaret Lemon, his passionate mistress, was not in the least pleased that Van Dyck should have rejected her to marry another woman, so she stabbed him. The painter's life was saved and he was able to rid himself of his furious mistress, but not without sustaining a wound in his right hand which could have left him badly mutilated.

Because of the disorders which were to lead England to civil war, Van Dyck returned to Antwerp, returning once again to London, but with the revolution gaining momentum, he decided to leave the country. He was unable to do so. A lung infection obliged him to remain in bed from August till December 9th 1641 when he died.

Piety, a painting which clearly shows the artistic virtuosity of Van Dyck.

The Metal Serpent by Anton Van Dyck.

In *The Capture*, Van Dyck depicts and intensely baroque atmosphere.

ver falsified the image of the people he painted with dishonest flattery. With an insuperable mastery he was able to captivate not only the soul of his sitters but also their basic character. He was unbeatable in portraying a likeness; his portraits are lovely but never contrived, always reflecting a basic reality. As a painter he was always interested in making his pictures vital and dynamic, which he was successful in doing superbly in his best works. His portraits are never static; they reflect life in their faces, in their clothes and in the atmosphere. Everything has vitality in Van Dyck's creations. Not only are his portraits of great quality but also his many self-portraits. The painter is consistent in approach and style in the self-portraits and uses the same honesty as in his portraits of others. He neither flatters his likeness, nor does he pretend false modesty.

Van Dyck is represented in the Prado by several magnificent paintings: *Sir Endymion Porter and Van Dyck, the Painter Martin Ryckaert, Charles I of England, Diana and Endymion surprised by a Faun, Capture*— a baroque apotheosis or The Metal serpent.

In *The Crown of Thorns* the artistic influence of Rubens is clearly perceived.

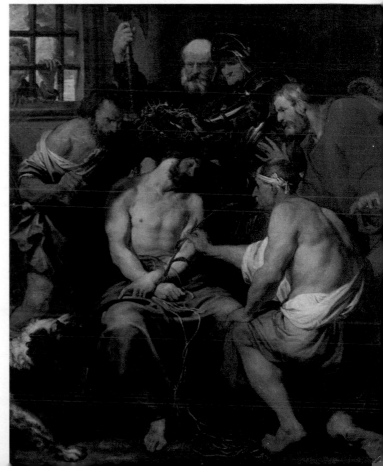

Van Dyck had the good fortune to live in a period which harmonized perfectly with his temperament, and to die when his creative talent was probably at its peak. His post at the court of Carles I allowed him to paint a series of pictures, basically portraits, showing his mastery of the speciality. His arrival in England at the time of Charles I was most opportune. His exquisite style of portraiture had to be successful at a court where an out and out dandy such as the duke of Buckingham dictated fashion with his lace clothes and affected ways. Van Dyck's baroque qualities suited Buckingham very well.

Without any doubt, Anton van Dyck was one of the greatest masters of the difficult art of portrait painting. It spite of his innate tendency to improve those he painted Van Dyck ne-

Portrait of Ferdinand IV by Luyck in the Prado Museum.

Doña María of Austria, Queen of Hungary, one of the portraits by Luyck on show in the Prado.

TENIERS

Both painters, Teniers the Elder and the Younger were named David. The Elder (1582-1649) painted several pictures on religious subjects, almost all of which were afterwards reproduced by his son. The father was unable to achieve much success as an artist. An unlucky man who started businesses for which he was probably ill prepared, he ended up in prison. His family was ruined and his son, Teniers the Younger, had to work hard in disadvantageous conditions to save his father from dishonour. He overcame all difficulties and achieved success, for at the age of 35 he was a much sought after painter.

David Teniers the Younger was born in 1610 in Antwerp and died in Brussels in 1690. He is one of the most Famous Belgian painters and is generally included among the most outstanding Flemish masters of the XVII century. He produced many works, there being more than 1,000 catalogued paintings of his. He painted on every conceivable subject and always with exquisity virtuosity. Among his best known works is *The Artist with his Family,* a picture depicting Teniers the Younger holding a lute and dressed as a gentleman. Around him are his wife, the daughter of Jan Brueghel, and their two sons. Everyone is beautifully dressed. The prosperity gained by David Teniers the Younger can easily be seen (the artist was about 35 years old at the time) in details such as the monkey accompanying the family and jumping onto the garden wall. The Archduke Leopold invited David Teniers the Younger to Brussels in 1651 and appointed him official painter and curator of his collection of paintings. The artist was highly flattered by this distinction. The poverty he had experienced because of his father's imprisonment had affected him in that it spurred on his ambition and vanity. But he was unable to obtain the rank of noble which would have been his dearest wish. Teniers the Younger was a pupil of his father's but rather better as an artist. His style was similar to that of Brouwer especially at the beginning. Later, however, he became more of a virtuoso, more conscious of his art. About 1640 he had evolved a very characteristic purified personal style. His subject matter was extremely varied. He painted on any theme, but on some rather more than others, tavern scenes for example, for which he used a subtle grey tone, or *The Temptations*

The painting entitled *The Archduke Leopold William in his art gallery in Brussels* by Teniers the Younger.

Village Festivity, by Teniers the Younger. Here the spontaneity of the scene in the foreground contrasts with the rhetorical tone of the landscape which is used as a back drop.

of St. Anthony which he situated in an impressive cave where fantastic apparitons were reflected, evidencing an extremely delicate use of colour. Among David Teniers the Younger's best known works are the following: *Peasant Dance, Pigeon Shooting, Teniers in front of his castle near Perck, Workshop, Winter Scene, Flemish meadow, The Archduke Leopold's picture gallery*, and *The Temptation of St. Anthony*. "David Teniers II, known basically as a stylist, says Philippe Daudy, is however, fundamentally a talented landscape artist. Successful counter lights, Dutch-style cloud effects alternate or at times give way to the subtle light of a landscape devoid of

any picturesque element. His use of colour becomes more simple, gradually reaching perfection, and some of his work archieves a poetry heralding Corot in its absence of superfluity".

The most interesting work of Teniers the Younger of those in the Prado is *The Archduke Leopold Willian in his Picture Gallery in Brussels*, in which works by Titian, Veronese, Giorgione and other painters are reproduced. Other works are *Drinkers and Smokers*, a painting of considerable strength, *Village Festival*, and *Smokers*.

Smokers and Drinkers and *Smokers,* two paintings of social customs by Teniers the Younger in the Prado Museum.

The Incredulity of St. Thomas
by Stomer.

Don Luis de la Cerda, IX Duke of Medinaceli, a protrait by Jacob Ferdinand Voet.

Hypomenes and Atalanta, an original work by Jacob Peter Gowi.

THE DUTCH SCHOOL

It would be sufficient only to mention the names of Hieronymus Bosch and Rembrandt for the Dutch school to enjoy a high level of prestige. But between the XV and XVIII centuries there were, besides the two painters of genius mentioned, a large group of Dutch painters of undoubted quality. The art movement of the so-called "Romanists", artists who studied profoundly the norms of Italian art and tried, in the words of Elie-Charles Flamand, "to transplant the new pictorical idea to their own country" was very important. This movement was parallel to that of humanism which also came from Italy and reached the Low Countries towards the end of the XV century, thanks to Rudolf Agricola and, a little later, to Erasmus. The Low Countries were the home of some of the most important publishers who played a key role in the propagation of the masterpieces of the Greeks and Romans and other humanist works, these were: the Elzéviera, Christophe Plantin and his son in law Moretus".

In southern Holland, the most important XVI century artist was Lucas of Leyden also called Lucas of Holland, who was also well versed in the technique of the great masters of humanism and is considered a precursor of the Dutch masters of the XVII century. Another important name is that of Jan Van Scorel, the first Dutch painter to go to Italy. "In Venice, wrote Flamand, he joined a group of pilgrims who, led by a Dutch priest were journeying to the Holy Land. After visiting the islands of Candia and Cyprus he reached Jerusalem where he was received by the superior of the Mount Zion convent. There he took notes from Nature which he was later to use for his landscapes". Scorel was a good portrait painter but outstanding as a painter of peaceful or fantastic landscapes, depending on his inspiration. Other recognized Dutch painters are Maerten Heemskerk, Antonio Moro, the nephew of Scorel and considered the best Dutch portrait painter, and Pieter Aertsen, with his markedly manierist influence, a painter of religious themes and works of style.

All Dutch painting is characterized by its peculiar use of light, by that unmistakable atmosphere which, already in the XVII century, filled the canvases of Pieter Jansz, Saenredam, Hals, Van Ostade, Metsu, Pieter de Hooch or Van Mieris Elder, and made Vermeer the basic element of a whole aesthetic approach.

The Skaters, by the Dutch painter Dubbols.

HIERONYMUS BOSCH

The date of birth of Hieronymus Bosch is not known with
any exactitude. Also known as "El Bosco" in Spanish, he was
one of the greatest and most singular geniuses of universal
painting. Whilst M. Gauffreteau-Sévy states that "no precise
document exists as a witness to his birth, this can be rea-
listically situated around 1450 or 1455, Elie-Charles Flamand
placing it between 1460 and 1465. Mario Bussagli, for his
part, states that he was born around 1450. J. Mosmans
tries to be more precise and points to October 2nd 1453 as
the date of birth of this great Dutch painter. What is certainly true is that there is no definite proof, and for the time
being it would be prudent to accept the hypothesis that this
disturbing artist was born between 1450 and 1460. J. B.
Descamps stated in 1600 that Hieronymus Bosch was born
in 1450 and at the end of the XIX century, Justi tried to re-
fute this, saying that the author of *The Seven Deadly Sins*
had come into the world in the year 1460.

It is by no means an easy task to reconstruct the personality of Hieronymus Bosch as a citizen and as a creature of
flesh and blood. His biopgraphy really underlies the complex
ambiguities of his painting. Precise information is lacking,
but there exists on the other hand, much hypothesis. Any approach to the life of the painter is based more on intuition
than on documentary findings.

Hieronymus Bosch's name was Jerome van Aken and it
appears he was the son of Anthonis of Jan van Aken. His
family, according to all indications was originally from
Aquisgran, but had settled, as Gauffreteau-Sévy states—in
Hertogenbosch "for many generations". A certain Jan van
Aken, a fur dealer who quite possibly came from Nimegen,
acquired the right of citizenship in 1399. Doubtless it is the
same Jan van Aken mentioned in the archives as the owner
of a house situated opposite the church tower, who died
in 1418".

What was Hieronymus Bosch's life like? How can he be
placed in the social context of his period and his country? What
was his way of thinking? What type of problems did he have
as a man and as an artist? These are always very difficult
questions to answer, and especially so in the case of the
gifted author of *The Hay Wain*. The key to the human personality of Hieronymus Bosch may never be completely revealed
unless one has recourse to unconvincing methods of an oc-
cult nature. It is not known who the masters who first orientated his artistic career were, or if they existed. It would
be logical to suppose that the father had influenced the
vocation of his son Hieronymus, but it would be false to
state that there existed a specific teaching by which Antonio
van Aken transmitted to his son what he had learned as an
artist. The documents in the Brotherhood of Our Lady reveal

There is a self-portrait of Hieronymus Bosch in this
fragment of the painting entitled *The Adoration
of the Kings*.

certain details of the life of Hieronymus Bosch. For example,
he worked as a painter in Hertogenbosch and died in 1516.
They also reveal that he was married before 1480 to Eleyd
van Mervenne.

It appears that the painter's wife belonged to a prosperous
family and brought him a substantial dowry. The documents
also state that around 1481 he finished off a triptych which
his father was unable to complete; this had been commissioned by the said Brotherhood of Our Lady which received
Hieronymus as an important member in 1486. As this in-

formation reveals, he lived comfortably, which partly explains, though paradoxically perhaps, the exquisite nature of his works. It can be argued that everything seethes disconcertingly in the art of Hieronymus Bosch. This is true. But the conflicting nature of his painting lies much more in its creative aspect than in its formal one. Hieronymus Bosch could have felt the anguish of spiritual and psychic contradictions but at the same time he experienced a vigorous sense of pleasure when painting. It is difficult to accept what Antonio Jorge Balcazar Morrison wrote on him. He states that "in spite of having lived at the beginning of the Renaissance, he was a mystic who was immersed in mediaeval influences. The multitude of beings filling his paintings are archetypes of exceptional symbolic value and transcendental meaning. His message is difficult for it is full of spiritual allusions at the same time." Hieronymus Bosch was

Two fragments of the famous painting entitled *The Garden of Earthly Delights*, one of the best known and most admired of the works by Hieronymus Bosch. The painting takes the form of a closed triptych and is done on wood.

The Adoration of the Magi is a magnificent painting highly representative of the technique of Hieronymus Bosch.

The Haywain, a triptych considered to have been painted during the early phase of Hieronymus Bosch's artistic development.

The Seven deadly Sins painted on a table top, is one of the finest achievements of Hieronymus Bosch. The surface of the painting is divided into seven parts representing Wrath, Pride, Lust, Sloth, Gluttony, Avarice and Envy.

much nearer to Jansenism than to mysticism. And anyhow, if in order to be a mystic, he had to renounce his sharp critical faculties (without which he would become dispossessed of one of his most characteristic qualities) his Jansenist rigidity would have been modified through his subtle sense of humour. The essential fact is that the personality of Hieronymus Bosch is basically contradictory and conflicting. His sense of humour often becomes acid sarcasm, especially when he vents his spleen and opens the gates of his heartfelt anticlericalism to mercilessly lash the hypocrisy of the clergy, while his esoteric qualities slide underground through a wide-awake sensibility and an overflowing sense of fantasy, joining, like a chronological river, the XV with the XX centuries.

Hieronymus Bosch had no children, his wife surviving him by some 10 years. The fact of never having had children could possibly have influenced the anguish often felt in his works. It was as if the painter, feeling that he was the end of himself and perhaps not believing in the resurrection of the flesh, felt a strong metaphysical urge to perpetuate in paint at least, the material and psychological pulse of human life seen through his own experience. This would partly explain the genesis of those motly worlds of flesh that invade the surfaces of his most characteristic works. In the painting of Hieronymus Bosch it is easy to perceive how his critical approach shows the folly of believing the world has been made for the uninterrupted enjoyment of the pleasures of the flesh. He was fond of placing the heads of pigs, dogs, birds or monkeys or any other animal on human bodies; in this way he symbolized the different vices inherent in human nature.

An artist of extraordinary personality, his vigorous approach to painting still astonishes us even today, five centuries after the inception of his unique work. The strength of the painting of Hieronymus Bosch lies mainly in the fact that, although he reacted clearly to the contemporary influences that inspired him, he opened out, almost miraculously, and became a herald of the invigorating advent of surrealism.

Hieronymus Bosch discovered the subconscious mind long before Sigmund Freud. This does not matter, or perhaps it matters a lot and in a positive sense, that such a discovery was made from an essentially artistic view point. The results are, in essence, very similar, Freud penetrated into the subconscious by means of psychoanalysis and Hieronymus Bosch did the same by expelling the devils from the human condition by depicting them in his creations.

As for technique, he is equal to the greatest painters of all time. Prodigious as a draughtsman, he worked with a minute and loving attention on his paintings. A great artist in miniatures at the service of a fabulous imagination. He painted as and what he wished and always succeeded in overcoming the many problems that beset him in every painting.

The perspectives in his landscapes are eminently Flemish, but always suffused by that unmistakable personal touch. Flat and static shapes are inserted nevertheless dynamically into the warm splashes of colour which give them life. Although the painting is always fantastic in concept and unrelated to a strict and conventional logic, human life flows

along, overflowing with vigour in the world of Hieronymus Bosch. In the Prado Museum there are many works of great value by this artist. The two most famous are perhaps those that should be mentioned: *The Garden of Earthly Delights* and *The Hay Wain*. The first is a closed triptych. An extraordinary work of art, it astounds us for several good reasons: its perfect execution, the veritable multitude of human beings and animals crowding the painted surface, the originality of its composition, the fantastic nature of its conception, the descriptive irony used by the painter, the rich colouring, variety of situations and the perfection of its narrative unity.

The Temptations of St. Anthony, a painting which is slightly different from Hieronymus Bosch's other works in colour and in execution, although the composition and spiritual atmosphere are clearly typical of his art.

The Extraction of the Stone of Folly, by Hieronymus Bosch. This work has four figures in the centre, one seated, another the demented patient, and the other two really no less demented surrounding the first figure. There is a landscape in the background and a superscription.

The Hay Wain, painted on wood like the former, is a triptych which when opened reveals the Hay Wain surrounded by the *Earthly Paradise* and *Hell,* and when closed shows the figure of *The Wandering Madman*. This is a profoundly dramatic painting. Even the use of colour reflects a dramatic tone, through the dark yellow apotheosis of the earth and the brightness of the illuminated air. The faces of the people depicted appear to be evilly suffused with the dark light of the most inconfessable passions. There is no humour, only implacable satire in this work.

The Moneychanger and his Wife, by Marinus van Reymerswaele (1493-1567).

St. Jerome, by Reymerswaele, a Dutch painting influenced by Dürer.

Philip II, a portrait painted by Heere; *Mary
Tudor, Queen of England, second wife of
Philip II*, by Anton van Dashorst Mor and
The Emperor Maximilian II by the same artist;
all these pictures appear in the Prado
collection.

A Sea Port,
by Parcellis.

A curious
snow covered
landscape by
Droochsloot.

REMBRANDT

Harmenszoon van Ryjn Rembrandt was a miller's son; his father Herman Gerritz was the owner of a mill near Leyden, a city to the south east of Amsterdam, and his mother Neeltgen Willemsd van Zuitbroeck the daughter of a baker. The painter's father lived quite comfortably. He had become converted to Calvinism and had married in 1599. The artist, fifth of the miller's six children, was born on July 15th 1606 and died on October 4th 1669.

The future painter was intended by his parents to enter the legal profession. While still a child he attracted their attention by the brilliance of his intelligence contrasting with the intellectual mediocrity of his brothers and sisters. Rembrandt studied humanities from 1613 to 1620. On may 20th 1620, he enrolled at the University of Leyden. But he was not fond of study and wanted to be a painter. He entered the studio of Jacob van Swabenburg after leaving the University. Later he spent six months in Amsterdam, at the home of the painter Pieter Lestman, and received his last lessons from Van Schooten.

He spent the whole of 1625 painting enthusiastically and immediately made his way as a painter in Leyden. He had many pupils, and his prestige as an artist grew considerably. Around 1631, became attracted by the idea of settling in Amsterdam, and associated himself with a painter and dealer, Heydrick Uylenburch, installing himself in his house. The following year he received a commission to paint his famous *Anatomy Lesson.* From then on Rembrandt began to live grandly. He was now an established artist, and there was no wealthy family in Amsterdam that didn't want to have a painting by him. His period of fame as an artist coincided with his falling in love. Rembrandt met Saskia, the daughter of a wealthy patrician at his associate's house and when her father died in 1624 leaving her an inheritance of 40,000 florins they were married. Saskia's presence was a good influence on the painter's life and he began to earn a lot of money with his paintings. Not many years later all this was spoilt when his wife died in 1635. Her relatives took up a lawsuit against Rembrandt whom they accused of being a wastrel. His painting underwent a deep transformation. Whilst the man retired from home life, the artist in him felt the need to reflect the world about him. Rembrandt kept away from society but drew nearer to nature.

Landscapes took over more and more of his canvas space. The happy man had gone and his conception of the world was occasionally slightly bitter. After Saskia's death, a critical spirit began to become apparent in his work.

Rembrandt's evident faithfulness to the real world constitutes a danger for the interpretation of his painting which appears to be easy to understand; however to do this is not quite so simple. It might be so if we limited ourselves to a superficial contemplation. Rembrandt did not manipulate reality neither did he idealize it gratuitously, he recreated it in a very characteristic way, developing as he painted, a process of poetic captivation of the world around and its profound meaning. The painter wanted to illuminate with the light of truth the real world buried under thick layers of frivolity and conventio-

nality of all types. Rembrandt endeavoured to bring order to the frivolous chaos of everyday reality. One of his most admirable successes as a painter lay in his ability to be able to paint a certain atmosphere. Let us take any of his paintings as an example of this, and examine that filtered light infusing the atmosphere of *The Syndic Drapers.* There is a spirituality in that picture that goes beyong reality, that makes it poetic in spite of the prosaic nature of the subject. This same personal concept of luminosity is shown in the most diverse of Rembrandt's works. It is unimportant that there is more or less light in this or that canvas. The atmosphere does not change except in degree, but in all of them there is the same inspired aesthetic motivation: the basic humanity of the atmosphere.

Two splendid examples of the art of this great painter are able to be viewed in the Prado: they are his *Self-Portrait*, a magnificent work, and *Artemis.*

In this *Self Portrait,* Rembrandt, one of the greatest portrait painters of all time, depicts his own face with an expression revealing his vigorous personality. The artist paints his likeness full face and wearing a turban with an air of looking more inward into his own world than at the harsh reality before him.

Artemis, an impressive work by Rembrandt.

Lady and Child by Adriaen Cronenburch.

HEDA AND VAN OSTADE

Willem Klaesz Heda was born in Haarlem in 1594, and died there in 1682. He was one of the best Dutch still life painters, and carried out his work at a time when large decorative pieces were being substituted for works of a lesser size and less sumptuous beauty. This taste was also prevalent in the sphere of painting and Heda interpreted it to perfection in his pictures where occasionally the themes introduced are the remains of a meal, a half empty glass of wine, and tin jug and a pipe, all of them objects grouped in disorderly fashion on a table. It was not a question of painting a table with the meal set out, but the memory of that meal. The *Still Life* by Heda in the Prado is representative of his aesthetic tendency.

Adriaen van Ostade (1610-1648) was also born in Haarlem and died there. One of the most popular Dutch painters, he enjoyed depicting peasant scenes full of movement. Van Ostade's style was impregnated with a vigorous irony and appeared to be influenced by that of his master, Hals, and also that of Rembrandt. The paintings belonging to his first phase are closely linked to the themes characteristic of Brouwer, who specialized in painting scenes of fights among villagers. Later, Van Ostade used his perspective, and painted subjects related to peasant scenes, with peddlers, organ grinders or interiors of poor-looking houses in which he tried to capture the atmosphere of Rembrandt's pictures. His work, *Villagers Singing,* in the Prado Museum reflects a facet of his approach to painting.

A magnificent *Still Life* by Willem Klaesz Heda, an artist who specialized in painting this type of subject.

THE GERMAN SCHOOL

Throughout the XIV century and at the beginning of the XV, the sphere of German painting was subjected to many influences. A concrete and definite style cannot be discerned, rather is it the coexistence of several styles struggling to gain precedence. "Every school, says Michel Hérubel, has its peculiarities: there are many regional schools very like the jig saw puzzle made up by all those states, half feudal and half bourgeois that constituted the Germany of that time. With all this it is possible to observe some characteristic that inspired German artists during the XIV century. Inspiration came from Italy with the frescoe painters; from France, with the miniaturists and cathedral sculptors; and from England with alabaster carving. To these three main European tendencies, two typically German influences must be added: that of Bohemia with its architectural and sculptural forms, and that of Westphalia with its intimite realism and direct simple humour well illustrated by the work of Maestro Bertram. Rhenish art, full of mystic potential, was excellent terrain for later receiving Flemish, and later Dutch influences". Painters representative of this period of German art are Lucas Moser, Konrad Witz, and Stephan Lochner.

Towards the end of the XV and at the beginning of the XVI centuries, German painting became free from extraneous influences and acquired a definite personality. At this time there appeared Dürer, Grünewal, Lucas Cranach and Holbein. The spiritual shock of Luther's reformation profoundly influenced the direction the concepts of German painting were to follow. "Parallel to this, comments Elie-Charles Flamand, "great economic activity was being developed, and Frankfurt, Augsburg and Nurenberg became important commercial centres, governed by a liberal and cultured patriarchy accustomed to great enterprises. This fruitful period brought forth some of the greatest painters in the history of German art. Although their work was always impregnated with "Gothicism", artists showed a growing interest for Italian art. In spite of its importance, the German Renaissance was, as has often been observed, but a brief episode occuring between late Gothic and baroque, developing after the Thirty Years War.

Charles V at the Hunt, a fine landscape in which Lucas Cranach reveals his exceptional gifts as a painter.

DÜRER

Albert Dürer is without any doubt the most vigorous personality of the German Renaissance. The jurist Cristopher Scheurl, professor of the University of Wittemberg, wrote to Lucas Cranach in a letter dated 1509: "With the exception of Albert Dürer... who cannot be compared to anyone, you should cetainly occupy the first place in the painting of this centuty". This statement is in no way an exaggeration.

Dürer was born on May 21 st 1471 in Nuremberg and died there in 1528. He learnt the goldsmith's trade from his father, and later had lessons in painting from Michael Wolgemuth. In 1490 he travelled along the Veneto taking notes from life. "Among the works he painted during his journeys, says Flamand, the most important of theim is a *Self-Portrait* on parchment dated 1493. As this picture was meant for his fiancée, he painted himself holding a blue thistle in his hand. (Thistle in German is *Männertreu,* meaning faithful husband.) The face, with its serious expression, in framed by long blonde curls, accentuating its delicate, almost feminine aspect". In 1494, he married Inés Frey and opened a studio in her parents' house. He painted several altar pieces and votive pictures and during this period he also painted among others, the following works: *Adoration of the Kings, Paumärtner Triptych, Apocalypse,* and *The Holy Family with a Butterfly,* the last two being engravings, one on wood, and the other on copper. He also did some interesting portraits such as those of *Hans Tucher* and *Frederick the Prudent.*

In 1505 he went to Venice and on his return to Nuremberg painted *Adam and Eve* and *the Martyrdom of the 10,000 Christians.* For seven years, frrm 1512 to 1519 he worked for the Emperor Maximilian I of Germany. An extraordinary engraver, he made 92 plates for *the Triumphal Arch* and also collaborated in the making of the 134 engraved tablets composing the *Triumphal Cortège of Maximillian.* His famous *Self-Portrait* — in which Dürer is painted wrapped up in a black cloak and with a pomegranete in his hand, dates from 1519, the year of the Emperor's death.

The following year there was an epidemic of plague in Nuremberg and Dürer went to Holland. He stayed successively in Antwerp, Brussles, Aquisgran, Cologne, Zeland, Ghent., Bruges and Malinas. On his return to Nuremberg he devoted himself to work on his last masterpiece: *The Four Apostles.* After this before he died, his *Treatise on the Proportions of the Human Body* and *Instructions on the Method of Measuring* were published.

With Dürer, German art reached its highest point. "Dürer, says Maurice Hamel, was one of the greatest men ever to honour humanity. An outstanding representative of the German race, he was above everything else, a universal genius. He participated heart and soul in the moral and

intellectual life of his time, in his doubts and in his achievements. These were too important for him not to have left moving images of them, but he was strongly attracted to the essential character of life and being, not to reach, at any point in time and space, all living men. The discovery of Nature; this was the clean task and heroic discovery of Dürer. He freed it from the past and made it devoid of all formalism; he is simply a man face to face with eternal matters. As regards form, the character he captures, it is not he who makes it more apt to please, but that he explains it better. What he demonstrates is his raison d'être the inner principle that supports it, the desire that animates and nurtures it. Thus, he gives us the feeling of the perpetual transformation of effort and of the aspiration of all things to

Unknown Gentleman, a splendid portrait showing the great quality of Dürer's work.

universal life. Dürer's style is the visible sign and the exact transcription of his emotion before all things. More draughtsman and engraver than painter, Dürer knew little of the musical value of tones and the song of colour. Drawing was his true language". His painting is certainly attached to his mastery as a draughtsman and does not reach with colour the profound dimension he always achieves in his engravings. Nevertheless, his importance as a painter is evident and his work as a landscape artist would be worthy of any artist of merit. This great German artist is represented in the Prado Museum by a magnificent *Self-Portrait, Adam and Eve,* and several other works, especially engravings. It could be said that it was the *Self-Portrait* that inspired these verses by Rafael Alberti.

Adam and Eve, the two famous tablets by Dürer enriching the Prado gallery.

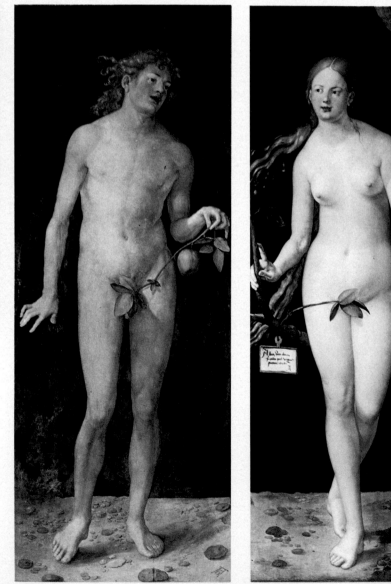

Pintor en cirugía,
paciente inquisitivo.
Tú, el angel pensativo
de la melancolía.

LUCAS CRANACH

Born in 1472 in Kronach near Bamberg (from where the painter took his name) Lucas Cranach-Müller or Sunder,— died in Weimar in 1553, and was one of the great figures of German painting. It appears he was initiated into the world of art by his own father who was also a painter. In Vienna, where Cranach's oldest painting, *St. Jerome with a Crucifix*, dated 1503, is kept, he came into contact with a group of Humanists who helped in the formation of his character. In 1504 he became court painter to Frederick the Prudent, he visited the Low Countries in 1508 and was a member of the Council of Wittemberg and a friend of Martin Luther who was godfather to one of his children. In 1547 when he was taken prisoner at the battle of Mühlberg, Cranach's protector, the artist Juan Federico shared his captivity in Augsberg. Among Cranach's best known works, mention must be made of: *Altar piece of St. Catherine, Altar piece of the Holy Family, Altar piece of Torgau, Rest during the Flight into Egypt, Mary with the Child, Portrait of Dr. Johannes Cuspinian, Portrait of Juan Federico, The Elector of Saxony, Venus, The Cortesan and the Old Man, Diana's Rest, The Nymph of the Fountain, Portrait of Luther,* and *Judith with the head of Holofernes.*

Lucas Cranach was as a man and as an artist constantly tempted by beauty, a deeply rooted humane beauty. "It is precisely to his extenuating search for the beautiful says Dora Schwarz, that Lucas Cranach devoted his lengthy career as an artist; a career with ups and downs, fervent creative moments and periods of exaustion. It is useless to look in this artist for the intellectual rigidity of Dürer, the passionate mystic ardour of de Grünewald or the solidly coherent style of Holbein. A mediaeval inheritance and Renaissance conquests, Germanic traditions and Italianate suggestions, asceticism and worldliness, Lutheranism and Catholicism, these were all component parts of his culture and his life, without his feeling the need to chose or to synthesize any of them. But from his work as a whole, so varied and often contradictory, there arises one of the most fascinating images of the great pictorical period of XVI century Germany".

In all the works of Lucas Cranach there is a sort of human vibration of emotion, not completely assumed by the intellect but with a powerful strength of sentiment, of contradictory struggle, aspiring and anguished that impregnates his best artistic achievements with poetry. There is a painting by Lucas Cranach in the Prado:—*Charles V at the Hunt* which is full of dynamism and with an evocative and subtle use of colour. Lucas Cranach, called the Elder, had two sons, Hans, the elder of these died in 1537, the other Lucas, the Younger, died in Weimar in 1586 and was also a painter of note.

Self-Portrait, one of the best paintings by Raphael Mengs in the Prado Museum.

MENGS

Raphael Mengs was born in 1728 in Aussing and died in Rome in 1779. He learnt to paint in Rome and Dresden and at the age of 17 was already a court painter in Dresden. He decorated the church of St. John in Rome and painted many portraits. In 1761 Charles III appointed him first court painter at the court of Madrid where he decorated the Royal Palace at the same time as Tiepolo. Later he went to Italy and returned to Madrid in 1773 where he stayed until 1777. In Rome he got to know Winckelman, and under his influence, became a sworn enemy of the rococo style. As a painter, Mengs was a rather shallow virtuoso. There are several works of his in the Prado: a *Self-Portrait,* and several other portraits among them one of *Charles III,* another of *Ferdinand IV,* king of Naples, and those of the *Queen Maria Amalia of Saxony,* and *Maria Carolina of Lorraine, Queen of Naples.*

Charles III, Ferdinand IV King of Naples, Queen Maria Amalia of Saxony and Maria Carolina of Lorraine, Queen of Naples, four works by Mengs in which he shows his ability as a portrait painter.

Wedding celebrations and country dance, a painting by Watteau on show in the Prado.

THE FRENCH SCHOOL

At the end of the XIV century, French painting had its main centres in cities such as Tours, Angers or Bourges. There was a mutual exchange of artistic influences between Burgundy and France; the France of Turenne had retired to the banks of the Loire due to military pressure from the English. Artists like André Beauneveu, Drouet Dammartin and Calus Sluter were those who kept the French art tradition alive. Among works of this period the following are outstanding: the series of tapestries of the *Apocalypse* by Jean de Bandol, the illustrations of the book *The Hours of Rohan, the Anunciation* at Aix, attributed to various authors, *Piety* from the Carthusian convent at Villeneuve-les-Avignon, now in the Louvre, by an anonymous author, a tablet which is an authentic jewel of XV century French art, *The Coronation of the Virgin,* a valuable work by Enguerrand Quarton, a fine exponent of the Paris school at that time, *The Virgin and Child* by Jean Fouquet, a tablet painted in oils, elegant in style with an expressive use of colour now in the Antwerp Art Museum, the *Resurrection of Lazarus* and the *Burning Bush* by Nicholas Froment, court painter to king René, or the series of portraits — *Charles of Bourbon,* for example, painted by the maestro de Moulins.

When Francis I acceded to the throne of France in 1515 the Renaissance gained great impetus. The young French monarch, who at that time was only twenty three was a cultivated intelligent and generous man under whose magnanimous patronage the plastic arts reached a period of brilliance. The rival of Charles I of Spain and V of the Holy Roman Empire in political and military fields, Francis I also wished to emulate him as a patron of the arts. A result of this rivalry in the sphere of art was the purchase of pictures by Leonardo da Vinci, Raphael, Titian and Andrea del Sarto, and the inception of the so-called Fontainebleau school founded by the French pupils of Rosso, Primaticcio, and Niccola dell'Abbate, — Italian painters invited to the court of Francis I.

However, the first French painter to be freed from the Italian influence was Jean Cousin who was not paid by Francis I nor was he one of the Fontainebleau school. "He was, says Elie-Charles Flamand, a provincial painter who in middle life settled in Paris where he worked freely and not under the immediate direction of the Italians. He was also a man of strong personality, comparable, in a way to Leonardo da Vinci or Albert Dürer. Indeed, not only was he a glass blower, painter, sculptor, engraver and architect but also a theoretician of some note." At the present time, there is only one remaining picture by this artist — *Eva Prima Pandora* which is, according to Flamand, a faithful reflection of his personality and at the time a perfect testimony of his art. The allegorical composition with its mixture

of the sacred and profane is representative of the spirit of the times".

Other French artists worthy of mention are, a son of Cousin's, also named Jean, whose masterpiece entitled *Final Judgement* gave him the nickname of nothing less than "the French Michel Angelo", and Antoine Caron one of the best known pupils of the Fontainebleau school who was court painter to Catherine de Medici and whose most important works are the series of the *Triumphs* and *the Meeting of Abraham and Melchizedek.* Painters from the Fontainebleau school were, among others, Ambroise Dubois, the decorator of the room where Louis XIII was born, Toussaint Dubreuil, author of the frescoes of the story of Hercules on a pavilion at Fontainebleau demolished in 1703, and of the paintings *Ancient Sacrifice* and *Woman Greeted by a Warrior,* Martin Fréminet, the excellent portrait painters Jean and François Clouet and Corneille de Lyon. Some works by anonymous authors of this period are also most interesting, such as the famous painted tablet entitled *Gabrielle de Estrée and her Sister, Triumph of Flora, Diana the Huntress,* and *Tepidario.*

The XVII century produced an artist of great importance in the history of French painting. This was Poussin. A cultivated man and reader of Descartes and Montaigne, Nicolas Poussin painted in a harmonious and strictly balanced style. In his book, *To Painting* in which he defined with his usual precision, the aesthetic quality of this French painter, Alberti also dedicated this poem to Poussin.

> *La razón se hizo pura*
> *plástica permanente;*
> *su sueño, la abstinente*
> *mano de la pintura.*
>
> *La forma iluminada*
> *que iba a volar se aquieta,*
> *claridad modelada.*
>
> *Los espacios licitan,*
> *luz y sombra, el lenguaje*
> *abierto del paisaje*
> *que los dioses meditan...*

Artists belonging to the same century are Claude de Lorraine, Louis Le Nain, Georges de la Tour, Philippe Champaigne and Simon Vouet. Later from the XVIII century are Antoine Watteau, Jean Honoré Fragonard, Louis-Michel Van Loo, Boucher, Chardin, Maurice Quentin de la Tour and many others. It was however, in the XX century when French painting really reached the peak of its brilliance.

VOUET

Simon Vouet went to Rome to learn to be an artist and was elected principal of the Academy of St. Luke in 1624. His painting developed from a baroque, close to Guercino,

The Virgin and Child with St. Isabel. St. John and St. Catherine by Simon Vouet.

Time conquered by Youth and Beauty, another of the paintings by Vouet in the Prado Museum.

Louis XIII of France, en excellent portrait painted by Philippe de Champaigne.

into a classicism influenced by Reni and Domenichino. Traces of the influence of Caravaggio can also be observed. From 1628, Vouet lived in Paris and was made a court painter to Louis XIII becoming for some years the most respected of French artists. The following pictures by Simon Vouet are to be seen in the Prado: *The Virgin and Child with St. Isabel, St. John and St. Catherine,* and *Time conquered by youth and Beauty.*

CHAMPAIGNE

Born in 1602 in Brussels, the French painter Philippe de Champaigne died in Paris in 1674. He began his career as an artist while still a child under the direction of Bouillon and later under the miniaturist Miguel de Burdeos. Champaigne was much influenced by the art of Poussin. In 1628 he was appointed painter to the Queen Mother Mary de Medici and later was court painter to Louis XIII, Cardinal Richelieu, Anne of Austria and Louis XIV.

Apart from Poussin's influence, there are traces of some Flemish painters in the work of Champaigne, especially of Rubens. Champaigne was one of the most prestigious portrait painters of the XVII century. He had a style of his own with greys and dark colours and a subtly balance light and shade predominating in his painting. In the faces of the people whose portrait he painted some of the author's melancholy character is reflected. One of his most famous works is that of two nuns, one of them his daughter Catherine and the other the Mother Superior Ines D'Arnault, in remembrance of the apparently miraculous cure of the former.

The Grand Dauphin by Charles Beaubrun.

Other works of importance by this painter are, *Louis XIII kneeling before Christ, Louis XIII confering the order of the Holy, Spirit on the duke of Longueville, Self-Portrait, Portrait of Cardinal Richelieu, Christ recumbent,* and *The Supper.*

Between 1640 and 1650, the painter was associated with the Jansenist religious sect and for the rest of his life worked for the nuns at Port-Royal where his daughter had taken vows. A sort of baroque classicism is the predominating note easily observed in this painting by Champaigne —*Portrait of Louis XIII of France,* now in the Prado Museum.

LARGILLIERE

Nicolas de Largillière was born in Paris in 1656 and died there in 1746. The son of a French businessman who settled in Antwerp, he learnt about painting in that city and later spent four years in England as the assistant of

Pierre Lesly who commissioned him to restore four old paintings at Windsor. He returned to Paris in 1678 where his name as an artist quickly acquired fame and he became the favourite portrait painter of the Parisien upper middle class. He was in contact with the painter Le Brun and protected by Louis XIV. Later he returned to England where James II commissioned him to paint his portrait and that of the queen and the Prince of Wales. He also did many portraits of people at the English court. His magnificent *Portrait of Le Brun* succeeded in gaining him membership of the Paris Royal Academy.

Among the most important works of Nicolas Largillière are those entitled, *Louis XIV, Colbert, The Cardinal of Noailles, Mlle. Duclos, Convalescence of Louis XIV, The Counsellors, Self-Portrait, Portrait of Voltaire, Marriage of the Duke of Burgundy,* and *Banquet given in 1687 by the city to Louis XIV.*

Portrait of María Ana Victoria de Bourbon by the famous French portrait painter Nicolas de Largillière.

Philip V, a work by Rigaud evidencing his ability
as a portrait painter.

Louis XIV, another characteristic portrait by Rigaud.

Nicolas de Largilliere's painting is characterized by its richness of colouring and by the agility of its execution. The
quality of his free baroque style portraits is undeniable. Van
Dyck's influence can be seen in them, and also that of Peter
Lesly. "Clear and bold tones, together with a scrupulous
technique, says Claire Gay, were of great use to him in
being appreciated by an elite of upper middle class people
whose importance at the beginning of the century was constantly on the increase. His superiority lay perhaps in his
ecclecticism; the delicacy of the use of colour, his clarity,
and an atmosphere of distinction heralding Watteau". The
Portrait of Maria Ana Victoria de Borbon in the Prado
Museum reflects these observations made by Claire Gay.

RIGAUD

A good collection of names precede the surname of the
French painter Rigaud y Ros: Hyacinthe-François-Honorat-
Mathias-Pierre-André-Jean. Born in 1659 in Perpignan,
Rigaud died in Paris in 1743. He was the son and grandson
of undistinguished painters. On coming to Paris in 1681
he was lucky in that his work pleased the painter Le
Brun. The following year he won the first prize for painting authorized by the Academy. Rigaud had begun by
painting pictures on historical subjects, but Le Brun per-
suaded him to leave that type of work and to devote himself
to portraiture. He took his advice and became one of the

The Family of Philip V by Jean Ranc, a French artist influenced by his compatriot Rigaud.

best XVII century French portrait painters. Among those whose portrait he painted were: La Fontaine, Bossuet, Racine, Boileau, Nicolas Coustou, Claude Hallé, Louis de Bolonia, Desjardins, the Cardinal de Polignac, Girardo, Santeul and Coysevox, one of his best ones being *Portrait of My Mother.* He also painted the crowned heads of France, Spain, Poland and Sweden.

In some of his works, especially in his portraits of kings, the influence of Van Dyck is to be observed, and in others that of Rembradt. Rigaud's painting constituted a link between the baroque of the XVII century and the moderate naturalism of the XVIII. Perpignan gave the artist a noble title in 1709 and he was appointed Rector of the University in 1733. Rigaud's mastery of portraiture is shown in his paintings of *Philip V* and *Louis XIV,* both in the Prado gallery.

RANC

Jean Ranc was born in Montpellier in 1674 and died in

1735 in Madrid. The son of Antonio Ranc who was also a painter, he was the friend and pupil of Rigaud and married a niece of his. In 1703 he was received into the Academy and admitted as a painter of historical subjects a year later.

Philip V summoned Ranc to Madrid in 1724 and there this French painter did several court portraits which is why the Prado Museum possesses a considerable collection of his works, among them, *The Family of Philip V.* In this collective portrait the king and queen of Spain are depicted surrounded by their relatives. Its composition is artificial and the use of colour is not outstanding. It has nervertheless some value as a historical document. Essentially it is a canvas very much in keeping with Rigaud's style, but without the artistic brilliance characteristic of his work. Another of the paintings of Jean Ranc in the Prado is the *Portrait of the Infanta Maria Ana Victoria.* It has that certain grace of a delicate miniature. The composition is as always in Ranc, contrived, but the expression on the little Infanta's face is subtly reflected in the picture and the colours are more muted than in others of his works. Similar objections can be made to the portrait

The Infanta María Ana Victoria, Charles III and
Philip V, three portraits by Ranc all of which are in
the Prado Museum.

of Charles III and perhaps with more justification as its
composition seems even more contrived than in the works
previously mentioned, and the use of colour more strident.
The same comment would be valid for the *Portrait of
Philip V.* In essence, his painting was very characteristic of
XVIII century French art, the whole of Ranc's work tending
to a virtuosity suffused with frivolity.

SILVESTRE

Louis de Silvestre was born in 1675 in Sceaux and died
in Paris in 1760. His initiation into the world of art was
first under the direction of his father, Israel Silvestre, himself a painter, and then under Charles Le Brun and Bon
Boullogne. Later, he studied further with Carlo Maratti in
Rome. On returning to Paris in 1702 he was received into
the Royal Academy. He became professor, rector, and
director of the Academy in 1706, 1748, and 1752 respectively.

Portrait of María Amalia of Saxony by the French painter Louis Silvestre.

Louis I by Miguel Angel Houasse.

Louis de Silvestre was appointed first painter to the court of Dresden in 1724 and painted the decorations on the royal palace at Warsaw, besides some rooms in the Zwinger electoral palace.

In his picture *Maria Amalia of Saxony* in the Prado, he offers an example of his ability as a portrait artist.

HOUASSE

Michel Angel Houasse was born in 1680 in Paris and died in Arpajon in 1730. Son of the painter René Antoine Houasse, both spent the greater part of their lives in Spain. Houasse was a painter to Philip V from 1717 to 1730. He painted mythological portraits and some interesting works on social customs, among these the following are outstanding: *Game of Bowis — Blind Man's Buff,* and *Tea on the Lawn.* These paintings were done to decorate La Granja. One of his pupils was the Spanish painter Antonio González Ruiz, court painter in 1756 and author of several cartoons painted for tapestries. M. A. Houasse was made a member of the Paris Academy in 1707. His ability as a portrait painter is shown in the work *Louis I,* now in the Prado Museum.

The Holy Family with St. John, another of the paintings by Houasse in the Prado gallery.

View of the Monastery of El Escorial, by Houasse.

In his *Festivity in a Park* Watteau
reflects that spirit of profound
melancholy apparent in the best of
his work.

Festivities in the Gardens at Aranjuez,
another painting by Watteau in the
Prado Museum.

WATTEAU

Antoine Watteau was a fashionable French XVIII century painter born in Valenciennes in 1684 and who died in Nogent-sur-Marne in 1721. A member of a well to do family of humble origins, he reached Paris in 1699 and lived for some time by copying paintings which he sold to a poor dealer on the Notre Dame bridge. Watteau climbed the artistic ladder with some difficulty until he was able to impress with the undoubted quality of his work.

He has been catalogued amongst the frivolous and sensual painters in the rococo style. There is, it is true, much frivolity and facile sensuality in Watteau's painting, but this is no impediment to the recognition of the quality of his art. Under the elegant appearance of his work there lies a deep melancholy. Watteau was actually a romantic who even suffered from tuberculosis and died at an early age in the typically romantic tradition. "Whether Watteau wanted it so or not, states Elie-Faure in his *Histoire de l'Art,* his sentimental comedy is, in the eternity of nature, the image of human existence, seen by an ardent human being through his bitter destiny. In it people constantly face an admirable love, a life too short and the unattainable infinite. A trembling soul, an adoring soul, faded roses and trembling pale blues like his withered existence. He feels he is about to die. And at his last breath his conscience awakes and premature repose expresses the happy appearance and cogent realities of the adventure to which he is condemned". In his work in the Prado Museum, the delicate melancholy

The Surrender
of Seville to
St. Ferdinand
by Flipart.

artistry of this great painter can be well appreciated.

His work is certainly not all erotism, but there is indubitably a certain amount of it. This is quite logical. We must not forget that Antoine Watteau was painting in France in the century of gallantry par excellence, when the French court made history in the boudoires of court favourites. But, underneath this veneer of frivolous erotism, under the appearance of a hedonistic type of gaiety, there exists in Watteau's painting a sad poetic sentiment. On the other hand, in his works an evolution can be observed which attenuates the brilliant tones in his paintings entitled *Embarcation for Cytherea, the Isle of Love* and subtly mutes the tone of his last works.

Outstanding among his paintings are: *Country Feast, Rest during a Hunt, The Judgement of Paris, Festivity in a park* (Prado) *Love Feast, Open air amusements, Dance in the Park, Village Wedding, The Angry Woman, The Indifferent man, Gilles and Colombine, Love in the Italian theatre, Love in the French theatre* and the famous *Gersaint poster*, done in three days.

There exists an undeniable charm in Watteau's painting. This pained longing to perpetuate the ephimeral passing of transient gaiety reflects the real personal drama of the painter himself.

A typical
Landscape
by Jean
Pillement.

Louis XVI, a portrait painted by the French artist A. F. Callet.

Other painters with works in the Prado are Van Loo, Louis Michel (1707-1771) who worked first in Rome and then in Spain where he was first painter to the king, some works of his are in the museum — *The Family of Philip V,* and *The Family of Philip V,* and *The Infante Don Felipe de Borbon, duke of Parma,* Flipart the author of *The Surrender of Seville to San Fernando;* A. F. Callet with his *Portrait of Louis XVI,* and Malaine with his *Flower Bowl.* These are works of uneven quality which represent, in the context of XVII century French painting a period full of artists and painters headed by such figures as Maurice Quentin La Tour, Jean Baptiste, Joseph Pater, Jean Honoré Fragonard, François Boucher, Jean Baptiste Simeon Chardin, Jean Marc Nattier, in addition to those already named.

Flower bowl, by the French painter Malaine.

PILLEMENT

Born in Lyon in 1728, Jean Pillement died in that same city in 1808. He was a much travelled painter who was successful in several different countries. A painter at the Polish court, he lived some time in Vienna and had great success with his several exhibitions in England between 1760 and 1780. He was also successful in making his way as a painter in the French capital where he painted for Marie Antoinette.

His work is extensive and embraces diverse themes, from landscapes to paintings of popular scenes, and also seascapes and flowers. He not only painted in oils but was also a talented water colourist, a good draughtsman and engraver. The *Landscape* in the Prado fully demonstrates the artistic ability of Jean Pillement.

THE ENGLISH SCHOOL.

The XVIII century was the most splendid period for English painting. "Proud and fertile, after a long period of lethargy, suddenly, says Claire Gay, it made a brilliant contribution to the artistic patrimony of Europe. Several different political economic and cultural circumstances had to arise for such an artistic flowering to manifest itself without losing its originality in the midst of a frenchified Europe. After the Treaty of Utrecht, it was the victorious and wealthy royalty who were prepared, following the footsteps of so many others, to participate in the great festivites of the spirit. Still poor in so far as native genius went, the England of Willian III, Queen Anne, George I and George II was content to welcome foreign artists. It gave commissions to the Italians Ricci, Amiconi, and Pellegrini. The stay in London of the two Canalettos was a real triumph. Philippe Mercier crossed the Channel in the wake of his protector the Prince of Wales and acclimatized there some "fêtes galantes" inspired by Watteau, who, in his turn undertook the same journey. At this time, English people went to study in Italy, passing through France, which engendered fruitful cultural exchanges. "English painting in the XVIII century up to the first quarter of the XIX century with Raeburn and Lawrence marked a late starting point. Its arrival coinciding with the era of prosperity that began in 1760 when George III a popular and cultured prince acceded to the throne. Well being, due to material wealth and to a state of peace gave way to an avid persuit of luxury and pleasure. All the rich of England travelled, danced, and had their portraits painted. Painting became the reflection of that society, described with humour or ferocity by some and glorified with elegance by others".

Nevertheless, it must not be forgotten that the true father of English painting was Hans Holbein, and later it was Van Dyck who made way for the great portrait painters like Thomas Gainsborough or Sir Joshua Reynolds. Holbein and Van Dyck were then, in spite of being foreigners, the two founders of English painting.

The great trilogy of XVIII century English portrait painters is made up of William Hogarth, Reynolds, and Gainsborough. Hogarth was the first English painter who dared to criticize the established order using his paint brushes. His work was basically didactic and to him is owed the evolution of English painting begun at the beginning of the XVIII century. His picture *Girl selling Shrimps* was considered by Whistler to be the best portrait painted by an English artist.

Reynolds exercised a decisive influence over the English portrait painters, and not only with his portraits but also with the popularizing of his theories. The outstanding position he occupied in the English artistic environment during his lifetime says Keith Roberts, was due to something deeper than his facility for creating a suitable image of the model: Reynolds was admired because in his paintings as in his public lectures on art (15 of them) he lent meaning to aesthetic principles in which his generation blindly believed. His canvases are not only images of a type of painting in which everyone wished to see himself reflected, they are also images and quite conscious ones of a XVIII century style and a defined attitude with regard to art." Reynolds himself stated in the 12th lecture: "The art of seeing nature, or in other words, the art of using models is really the great objective of the painter, the point toward which all his studies are directed". To the achievement of this "great objective" Reynolds meticulously adjusted the coordination of his art. The case of Gainsborough is somewhat more complex. "Gainsborough, observes K. Roberts, only wanted to be a landscape artist, but circumstances did not allow this, as he had to realize, and like Reynolds, accepted the fact, that to be able to live in England a painter had to practice the art of portrait painting. Gainsborough's true leaning was however amply demonstrated. Nearly all his early works are indeed landscapes, executed according to the minute formulae of the XVIII century Dutch painters; and later on he made constant allusion in his letters to the "damned portraiture" which stopped him from devoting himself to landscapes as he would have liked. In portraiture, the delicate acuteness of observation that characterized Gainsborough's youthful style is added to a more spontaneous touch, richer, and more carefree which is a sort of premonition of the more advanced stage of his artistic development.

A close examination of the later portraits can reveal the influence of Van Dyck and the results of the efforts of Gainsborough himself to improve his style and to make it more agile. During his last years, his painting gradually assumed more fragile tones. His technique became progressively freer like that of Velazquez, but while the dense brush strokes of the Sparniard came from his strict composition and style and gained a particular consistency, almost a bodily presence, the strokes of Gainsborough appear to vanish in the overall effect; this partly explains the ethereal and weightless quality of his later works".

William Turner was to be the painter who in the XIX century (1775-1851) realized Gainsborough's frustrated dream: to transform a landscape into the fundamental inspiration of English painting. Turner travelled in Germany, France and Italy. In Venice he painted extraordinarily beautiful views of the city and its canals. He was an excellent portrait painter, a magnificent engraver and an artist of genius in the use of water colours. Nobody has yet been able to better him in the poetic re-creation of a landscape. Turner is the landscape artist par excellence.

LAWRENCE

Sir Thomas Lawrence was born in Bristol in 1769 and died in London in 1830. At an early age he began to do work in pastels and drawings for the guests in the hostelry kept by his father. In London he was helped by Reynolds and quickly became successful. He was elected member of the Royal Academy and, on the death of Reynolds, appointed portrait painter to the king.

Lawrence went on several journeys through Europe and painted the portraits of the Emperors of Austria and Russia, and also of the Pope and Metternich, the Duc de Richelieu and other celebrated persons of the time. In England, his best portraits are those of Scott, Lady Blessington, Canning and Southey. Sir Thomas Lawrence, through he did not reach the rank of Reynolds or Gainsborough, can be considered an important artist.

John Vane, X Earl of Westmoreland and *Miss Martha Carr*, two characteristic works by the famous English portrait artist Sir Thomas Lawrence.

Contents

The printing of this book was completed
in the workshops of FISA - Industrias
Gráficas, Palaudarias, 26 - Barcelona
(Spain)